My Life in
Sarah Palin's
Crosshairs

DEER
IN THE
HEADLIGHTS

LEVI JOHNSTON

A TOUCHSTONE BOOK

Published by Simon & Schuster

New York London Toronto Sydney New Delhi

Touchstone
A Division of Simon & Schuster, Inc.
1230 Avenue of the Americas
New York, NY 10020.

First Touchstone hardcover edition September 2011

For information about special discounts for bulk purchases,
please contact Simon & Schuster Special Sales at
1-866-506-1949 or business@simonandschuster.com.

The Simon & Schuster Speakers Bureau can bring authors to
your live event. For more information or to book an event contact
the Simon & Schuster Speakers Bureau at 1-866-248-3049
or visit our website at www.simonspeakers.com.

Designed by Joy O'Meara
All interior text photos courtesy of Zach Cordner

Manufactured in the United States of America

10 9 8 7 6 5 4 3 2 1

Library of Congress Cataloging-in-Publication Data

Johnston, Levi.
    Deer in the headlights : my life in Sarah Palin's crosshairs / Levi Johnston.
        p.   cm.
    "A Touchstone book."
        1. Johnston, Levi.   2. Johnston, Levi—Childhood and
youth.   3. Johnston, Levi—Relations with women.   4. Palin,
Bristol.   5. Palin, Sarah.   6. Wasilla (Alaska)—Biography.   7. Wasilla
(Alaska)—Social life and customs.   I. Title.
    F914.W3J64   2011
    979.8'052092—dc23
        [B]   2011027810

ISBN 978-1-4516-5165-2
ISBN 978-1-4516-5167-6 (ebook)

Woke up this morning, what do I see? Three
thousand cameras, pointing at me

> "Levi Johnston's Blues"
> —Ben Folds and Nick Hornby

CONTENTS

DEER
IN THE
HEADLIGHTS

INTRODUCTION

You betcha, **she said,** smiling, when I asked if I could come in out of the snow to wait for Bristol.

Sarah really used to say that, all the time. It's the only authentic part left from her life before she was governor, before her failed national campaign, before Fox TV. Before my relationship with Bristol fell apart.

Sarah had welcomed me into her family back then; she'd called me her best friend. But as soon as I no longer fit into her oh-so-carefully-crafted moment in the spotlight, I was looking at the undercarriage of her campaign bus.

When I was a home-schooled freshman going over to Bristol's, Sarah was often the only one home. As a twelve-year-old playing hockey with Track Palin, I'd called her "Mayor Palin." Now, when I did, she waggled her finger.

Levi, you don't have to call me Mayor.

How about Mrs. Palin?

She smiled and shook her head. Sarah, she said.

When I entered the Palin home on those high school

1

afternoons, she would be in her favorite spot in the living room, on the leather sofa. She always had on a sweatshirt and PJ bottoms with silly little characters. She'd pat the cushion next to her for me to join her.

Sitting there, Sarah and I would talk about the kids, her clothes, and her Wasilla pals from years ago, the Elite Six, who met for lattes at Kaladi Brothers Coffee near Chimo Guns. She'd tell me about the home shows she followed on TV, and the soaps.

Sarah kept me from getting bored.

She acted like she loved me. I don't mean romantically— like a son. She used to call me that: *my other son.* One night when Bristol and I were up in her room, my babe said, I think my mom likes you better than me.

I just couldn't understand when down the road everything fell apart. *I still don't.*

Las Vegas, Nevada:
Happy Birthday to You . . .

You wouldn't think Alaska and Las Vegas have a lot in common—but they do. In both places, it's tough to know whether it's morning or the middle of the night. Inside the hotels and casinos of Vegas, it's like the sun is always shining. Lights burn around the clock and there aren't windows to give you some clues.

In Alaska, there's also a false daytime—for the part of the year when the sun never totally sets. You can wake up in Wasilla and start frying eggs and browning reindeer sausage thinking it's breakfast time, then find out it's only 2:00 a.m. It's like there's one of these Vegas showtime spotlights on your bedroom window all night long.

In both places, everything is over-the-top. Alaska has a park called Denali that's larger than Massachusetts. Vegas has sky-blue limos like the one I'm riding in. It's the size of a tank, and I'm sitting next to a guy named Tank. His real name is Sherman. I kid you not. He's my ginormous manager and bodyguard, and he's taking up most of the space as he waves his ham hock arms around telling me how awesome this party is going to be.

It'll be packed, he says, pointing a kielbasa thumb at the Chateau Nightclub & Gardens we're pulling up to.

It is going to be great. Just be yourself and everything will be fine.

He slaps me on my thigh. My upper leg goes numb.

He and I have just been delivered to yet another fifteen minutes of fame. I'm here to celebrate my twenty-first birthday, Las Vegas–style, at the nightclub of the Paris Las Vegas hotel and casino. Tank has told the press it's going to be insane, but a class act nonetheless. No strippers. None at all. Then of course he backslides. We'll see, he says.

He's ridiculous. He's got me primed for the reporters who've been cleared to interview me. He tells me what I should say, but he doesn't go on about what I shouldn't. It's all about the buzz, he says. I know the club has instructed the press not to ask questions about Bristol Palin or Sarah, my never-to-be mother-in-law. I think Todd is okay but I'm not sure.

Tank leaps out of the car as fast as a three-hundred-pound guy can and lumbers around so he'll be there when the driver opens my door.

I'm squinting into the spotlights as I step onto a red carpet. Several B-list celebs are already inside. I'm the last to walk the runner. I'm the star attraction. Levi posters are all over the place. This is my birthday. Twenty-one. The last year you really count. And the one that means I'm an adult.

Tank says the club will be packed with two thousand partygoers. I don't buy that. I do expect tables of cougars mixed with girls dressed in $400 jeans and skimpy tops. I've been here before, in Manhattan, Hollywood. I know the deal. These fans will want turns sitting on my knee, posing as their friends take photos.

From outside, standing on the red carpet, I hear music pulsing through the open doors. *North to Alaska* . . . The MC standing right next to me self-corrects his posture. He's wearing an electric-blue tux. He checks out my open-collar, plaid shirt, Hugo Boss jacket, and pressed jeans, then holds one arm straight out over my head as he roars into his mic:

H-e-r-e's LEVVVIIIIII JOHNSTON, folks!!!

His words, loud enough to carry halfway to Anchorage, make me think of my mom. Three short years ago she was screaming her heart out the same way—LEVVVIIIIII!—when I scored in high school hockey games. When she wasn't there in the stands, the coaches would ask, Where the hell is your mom? We need her here to help us win.

I'm scoring tonight in a vastly different venue, for less than pure reasons. I'm getting paid $20,000 for showing up. The MC tells the fans lined up on each side of the red carpet—people I've never met—what they already know, that I'm turning twenty-one, right here, right now . . . even though my birthday was three days ago.

There's a cheer and the MC turns to hold the mic nearer to me as the media presses in.

A blonde with a great smile approaches.

She looks at my manager, now functioning as my body-guard, then back to me. She asks, Have you seen Tripp?

I feel myself come alive. Yes, I say. I had seen my toddler son recently.

He saw him recently, my manager echoes.

She offers to buy me shots inside to celebrate my birthday. She would later post on a political blog that I blushed and looked at Tank for help. That's probably right. I don't do shots and didn't know what to say.

Are we going to like your book, Levi? She smiles.

You're going to *love* it, I say back.

My manager says, You're going to *love* it.

Is it going to tell what you know about Trig? Will you describe what it was like to pose for *Playgirl*?

I think, but don't say, that I can't answer these questions out of context, without their history. Without my own story—how I got to where I am today. That needs to come first.

Is the book done? I'm asked.

I'm on it, I say. It still needs a little work.

So does the rest of my life.

1

North to Alaska

If John Wayne hadn't agreed to play Sam McCord, where the hell would I be today? His film and the Johnny Horton theme song, "North to Alaska," were big hits back in the day, in 1960.

North to Alaska, go north, the rush is on. . . .

The movie was made in celebration of the Last Frontier's statehood. My grandpa Joel Johnston saw it and, then and there, decided he was moving. Way north. To find gold, he told me. I swear to God. Before he died, I bought him the DVD of the movie and he just about cried.

That John Wayne movie—three guys strike it rich—had set the Johnstons on the right path for the wrong reason. Both my dad and my grandfather loved the glorious state of Alaska just for itself. They hunted together; they fished; and panned for gold. Both loved books and, of course, films. Grandpa Joel was crazy about John Wayne. So is my dad Keith—and so am I.

In the decade following the film, four families—Palins and Heaths; Johnstons and Sampsons—found themselves

9

settled in Alaska. I don't think anyone could have predicted how this would end.

My then teenaged dad ended up graduating in Anchorage, from Dimond High. I always hated that school; they used to beat my hometown hockey team, Wasilla High.

My dad and my mom, Sherry Sampson, met in 1986 in Wasilla, an hour outside of Anchorage.

As a teenager, Mom started working at one of the beauty parlors her mother, my grandma Myrna, owned, the one called E-Z Clippers. One afternoon Dad walked in. Mom, who says she checked out this tall handsome feller without missing a snip, gave him an extra-long shampoo, then a scalp massage. She then trimmed and shaped his hair, dragging it out as much as she could.

Keith and Sherry married twelve months after that first shampoo and cut. I was born in 1990, and my kid sister, who in a nod to my grandmother was given the Mexican-American name Mercede, showed up eighteen months later. Mom always cut all our hair; she still does mine and Mercede's. Dad's, not so much. In fact not at all anymore.

All was great back then with the newlyweds. Dad, an electrician, used to have to travel outside Wasilla for jobs in Native villages. He'd be hired by contractors for six to eight weeks at a time. His employers boarded their construction workers in rooming houses. My dad had a different idea. He brought along our camper, and we'd choose a site to set it up, on a river or lakefront. It was like a summer vacation. When his job was done, we'd all go back to our house in Wasilla.

It was also in Wasilla that Sarah Heath met Todd Mitchell Palin, in high school. Up until then, Todd went to school in his hometown of Dillingham. He moved to Wasilla for his senior year.

After graduation he and Sarah took different paths. She would go off to colleges, while Todd ended up with a job on Alaska's oil-rich North Slope. He worked for BP—and he would also run a snow-machine business with a partner.

Once Sarah graduated, she and Todd married, in 1988.

My mom and pop stopped at two offspring; the Palins kept going. Track, fourteen months older than me; Bristol, a half year younger than I am; then Willow and Piper. A second son, Trig, was last. Both families were doing their part to grow the population of our small bedroom community.

Bristol Palin, Todd and Sarah's oldest daughter, and I would do the same. In December of 2008, she and I became parents to a son, Tripp Easton Mitchell Johnston. My goal was to bring up Tripp as an Alaska boy, just the way I was raised. As my grandpa Joel and my dad, Keith, would tell me, things don't always turn out the way you plan them to.

———

The Johnston and Sampson males introduced me to God's country. These days much of male bonding is done in tricked garages and basements and walking in malls. Back when I was growing up, at least in Alaska, no one needed to talk about what they were doing and why. They did it, always with their boys—teaching the upcoming wave of kids to read the woods and predict where the next rainbow trout might rise to a fly.

I have a mounted fish in my living room that brings those years back. I caught that lunker when I was a little older than my son, Tripp, when my dad took me fishing. I felt that trout's weight and knew the hook was set. So I turned and, without reeling in, put the rod on my shoulder and walked back up the bank. There's a video of that day and you can hear sniggers in the background, but they didn't last long. My grown-up relatives shut up when a fish appeared from the water behind me and plopped on the ground.

Wow, they said. God damn.

My mom's brother Robbie Sampson and my dad's cousin Huck Johnston still talk about that day. I love to point out that it *was* a trophy catch. A serious fish, even for an adult. They still laugh.

When I speak of it, it's like I can still feel the heft of that trout and the pride. I might have been a shrimp, but

I was one of the guys. I'd been accepted into the brotherhood.

My male relatives, the hecklers, were ballsy, somewhat crazy, and still are. Not in a *Deliverance* kind of way though. They wouldn't think twice about running a wild river in a canoe, catching air on a snow machine, jumping four-wheelers, or flying off hilltops 120 feet downslope. These same men had unending patience as they taught us boys what we needed to know to be out there, on our own and safe.

When we got home the day I hooked my fish, my dad pulled out his fillet knife to gut my first catch. He called me over to split the belly.

No, I yelled when I saw what he was up to.

Mom and Mercede—we called her Sadie—had stayed home that day. Whether they'd been on the adventure or not, the Johnston women prepared whatever was brought to them. I saw it as a signal to me when my mother reached up to take her cast-iron skillet off its hook. I was in charge of dredging the pieces of fish in a mixture of cornmeal and flour with a shot of cayenne. Then she'd fry them, and although I've eaten in some fancy places, I have still never tasted anything as good as my mom's fried fish.

For this fish though I wanted something different than dinner. Dad and I took my first trout to Foster's taxidermy the next day, and it still hangs on the wall above my living-room bay window for all to see. Seventeen inches of fish.

Almost eighteen. Maybe even bigger. One of Tripp's first words when I carried him into my house was a slobbery *fsshhh* as he pointed above his head and watched my face. I laughed.

When I was a few years older than Tripp, Dad and two or three of my uncles would heft me and my cousins into a couple of trucks and we'd be off. I had a plaid hunting shirt I wore until the cuffs just about touched my elbows. I loved it; it was like the grown-up shirts on the men.

I'd sit squished in the truck between an uncle and my father, the rub of my flanneled shoulder against the bulging arm of Dad's six-foot-three frame. The cab was full of the smell of men—wet leather, Red Man dip, gasoline dripped on the outside of the red fuel cans in the truck bed. When the weather was warm, we kids sat in the back on tackle boxes and spare tires, tickling one another when we slowed down, bumping into the cooler.

These are the kinds of memories I want my son to have. When he gets older, I'll be bringing him along on these outings, continuing the traditions of generations of Johnstons. I've already taken him fishing, and it was such a cool thing, watching him do just what I did as a kid, and seeing him as my father must have seen me. He splashed and played, not caring about the catch. The little guy carried his rod on his shoulder back and forth to the truck, watching my reactions to see if he was doing it the right way. After he was born, I bought a flannel shirt just like mine, in a kid's size four. He is still too small to wear it; it's hanging in the playroom closet next to his little ice skates.

Every male in Alaska used to live to fish and hunt. Times have changed. Todd Palin, Track's dad and Tripp's grandpa, isn't a serious hunter and neither is his son. I've heard that Track went out not so long ago and maybe did get a bear. Bristol, Track's sister, had mentioned that to me. It was the first time I'd ever even heard of him hunting. There aren't animals, live or dead, around the Palin house. One time at the dump, Sarah's parents, the Heaths, saw someone throwing away a caribou skull. Oh, can we have it? they asked.

The Palins are typical of today's Alaskan families: sport for them is more racing through, than being in, the wilderness. Track went snow machining with his dad now and then, and they commercial fished together in the summer. Other than that, the Palin men didn't have the relationship to one another and to the land that for me and my father was like religion.

When I was five years old, Dad gave me my first gun, a new single-shot .410 shotgun. Dad showed me how to clean and oil it. He kept my shells buttoned up in the top pocket of his shirt. We drove to Eureka, then up into the mountains looking for ground squirrels. I got tired of carrying my firearm. A half hour later and a half mile away, my Dad said, Where's your gun?

I set it somewhere.

So we spent all damn day looking for that gun. We ended up finding it leaned against a rock. Oh, God, did my dad yell at me.

I learned my lesson.

I still have that gun.

2

Son of the North Star

When I was in elementary school, my mother was the Kool-Aid mom. All my pals came to my house after classes. She'd always have snacks and drinks waiting. My dad flooded a hockey rink on our property year after year that was packed all winter with my buddies and my sister's, too. Track was one of the crowd, and every so often he, one of a bunch of ragtag kids, would stay for sleepovers. Not one of my good friends, though, like Matt Craver, Dom Nickels, Crosby, Chad, Tyson Sampson.

All my buddies were crazy about my mom and my pop. They were involved parents, no matter what I was doing.

Only a few years later my dad let me know he considered me to be responsible. I was in junior high, and the unspoken understanding between us was that I was good on my own, no matter what I ran into. I knew enough to know what I didn't know. He had always told me that was important.

That didn't mean he was no longer a part of my life.

To this day, he can drive me out of my mind with voice mails. In the end, however, he leaves my life up to me. At times my father rode my ass. He called me all kinds of shit, depending on his mood. Numskull, idiot—and worse. I thank him for it, now.

My dad always made sure I had the gear I needed, the stuff we refer to as toys in Alaska. Guns, tents, rods, spinning reels, and, for hockey, helmets, face masks, pads for my shoulders, elbows, and shins. Big honking gloves. Warm-up stuff. Skates for my feet and a uniform up top.

My dad gave and expected me to perform 100 percent. He rode me so hard to play high-level hockey that I once took $2,000 worth of gear he'd bought for me and threw it on the top of the burn pile. He made me go out, get it all, clean it, and put it away.

I was pissed but learned to pay attention to his advice. Those times when I didn't listen, it came back to bite me in the butt. It still does—but I've not been real good at remembering that for the last few years.

When I was growing up, he was my dad; now it's more a buddy relationship. I trust him, and he's still the first person who would come to mind now if I were to draw a Kodiak brown-bear tag—the pass that gives me the right to hunt on that island-world southwest of the Kenai Peninsula.

Kodiak is the second-biggest island in the United

States; only Hawaii's Big Island is larger. The Island of Hawaii isn't inhabited with brown bears; Kodiak is brown-bear heaven. They grow bigger there than anywhere else in the world. These beasts aren't managed like herd animals; density is maintained through the number of tags issued to hunters. Wildlife biologists estimate there's a bear on every one and one-half square miles of range. Kodiak Island is 3,500 square miles so that's 2,333 brown bears.

This part of Alaska is their house. These bears are ten feet tall, the King Kongs of the bear world. They grow to fourteen hundred pounds, the bulk of eight men. Their noses are damn long.

Even when you don't see them, they're there. They come at you on all fours. We're the slow-moving ones. Their eyesight is better than ours and their hearing is as good as a dog's. Their sense of smell is four times that of a bloodhound. These guys aren't stupid. I know what they can do to me and they do, too.

I'd always wanted to test my nerves by hunting Kodiak with a bow and arrow—but only if my dad had my back with his rifle. When I finally did draw a tag and Dad couldn't make it, I hunted with a muzzle-loader—a black-powder, single-shot weapon. Bow or muzzle-loader, I would only have one shot. With the muzzle-loader, I'd be farther away, safer than with a bow and arrow. More of a challenge than with a rifle.

On that last trip, me and Dominic Nickels—so close a friend that we're like brothers—packed our huge hunters' packs with one thousand pounds of gear for a one-week outing. We brought along someone I knew and liked from L.A., who had never hunted for anything anywhere before. We put together clothes, ammo, tents, stuff sacks, weapons, emergency supplies, satellite phones, GPS. We drove it all out to Anchorage to ship to Kodiak. Then we three guys jetted to the island and hooked up with our backpacks out there. Once on the island, we took a float plane that dropped us off at Deadman Bay. None of this was cheap.

There were no roads. No people. If we got in trouble, we were in trouble; we were not going anywhere. I would only go out there if I knew when and where I was being picked up. There was no room for error.

We brought along freeze-dried food packets that we would heat on our collapsible camp stove. Freeze-dried noodles and chicken. Freeze-dried breakfast skillet. Freeze-dried blueberry cheesecake, sandwiches, and cooked shrimp. Although that cheesecake turned out to be pretty good, we weren't out there for the eats. For the brown bears though, this area was like a huge buffet: salmon from the rivers and berries from the mountainsides, carrion—and any humans who pissed them off.

I know who I am from hunting. It's my identity—a world and an activity I know as well as anyone. Better. It's a place where I can survive.

Kodiak brown-bear country is different from the heavily treed home of black bears near Wasilla. Kodiak land is mushy, swampy in the valleys, with alder that has been stunted by the wind, the cold, and the fog. The saplings are ten, twelve feet high. Sometimes you can see the tops of these thickets trembling as a bear pushes through, on the move. You guess the direction and cut that bear off or you'll lose it.

My elbow cousin Dom and I had a silent communication, like twins, because we'd been doing this together for so long. Dom's dad was my dad's number one hunting partner. Dom and I grew up hunting with them, so he had the same experiences I did.

No matter how connected we are, Kodiak isn't our comfortable home turf. The bears live out there year-round. They don't just fly in for a week. They know what they're doing. If we hear as much as a twig snap, Dom and I are alert. We know something is messing around in there. We protect each other and get ready for the worst.

On that trip with the L.A. pal, we all were walking in, careful and quiet. We heard but could not see something ahead. We got closer and closer. Suddenly, around a turn in the game trail we were following, there was a bear, hunched over, head down. He was grunting quietly. Then he picked up his head and stood. He puffed up, trying to scare us, and stomped his rear paw on the ground. *Whop.*

The California guy started to quiver. Maybe moaned.

He'd been between us; now he took a step back behind Dom and froze, not knowing what the hell was going to happen.

The bear perked.

This wasn't a big bear. Dom and I knew we didn't want to shoot him. We had a moment of indecision, as did the bear. He started to charge and we aimed. Just as Dom and I began to squeeze our triggers, the bear changed his mind. Turned and walked away.

It took the third member of our team about a week to calm down. We've invited him to come up again, but we haven't seen him back yet.

If you don't bug them, most Alaskan bears are like the one Dom and I and the L.A. guy ran into. Live and let live. This had been the unofficial motto for Alaska's hard-bitten citizens, too, for many a year. Back when there was a lot of room between tar-paper shacks. Once a few more of us were up here with actual settlements, everyone started to mind everyone else's shit. The flip side of this and the part I like to focus on is that everyone also knows when someone needs help.

People like my family and the Palins lived out the rugged life they dreamed about before they moved to Alaska. I grew up in a house that, like my friends' places, was more or less square, on similar pieces of land. Our plot was tucked away in a subdivided tract cut out of the woods. My folks could have afforded a nicer place in a better location, but my dad loved his toys and wasn't about to spend money on what he saw as frills. He'd lay out thousands on hunting equipment, a boat, the newest truck. Not a house.

Our three-bedroom bungalow had a bathroom, a living room, and an eat-in kitchen. Dad had painted the outside gray, and wired it.

The Palins lived a ten-minute bike ride away from our house—in a green, tin-roofed house. It was bigger than ours, but not so very different.

The Palins and the Johnstons lived in similar houses—and our politics weren't all that different either. Until they changed. There had been a constant quiet battle in town between those who wished to leave things the way they were like my parents, and newer residents who wanted to keep up with the Joneses and needed department stores and the newest fast foods. I was six when Sarah Palin became our mayor. Her support came from those who wanted the town to grow. More businesses; fewer regulations. More population.

Once these new folks had settled in, they tried to make Wasilla like what they'd left behind—because it was what made them comfortable. They were looking for opportunities for themselves and their children. The pro-growth folks pushed hockey for the kids—and for themselves—during the long winter months.

The larger world had Little League, Pop Warner football, and soccer moms. Wasilla had hockey, Mini Mites to semipro, and hockey moms. In my case, a hockey mom and dad.

My parents came along to see me play in these organized games. Mom, who knew all the players, would root for me and all my friends even when they were on the opposite team. I can still see her in my mind, jumping up and down, from back when I was an elementary-school kid—even though she was usually sick.

3

A Dog Named Ice

It took years for the docs to finally figure out what was wrong with Mom: her body couldn't use the vitamin C it needed, so she had developed scurvy, a painful joint problem. It makes you think of old sailor stories. It was an awful thing for her. Aside from the damage the scurvy caused, she was left with a mess of scar tissue and nerve damage from the exploratory and correcting operations removing this and that. She couldn't keep up the beauty-parlor business, so she did what she could out of our house. Eventually she became too disabled for even that. She wasn't a complainer, even though it wasn't an easy ride for her.

In 2003, when I was in seventh grade, my dad had started work on the Slope, for the Arctic Slope Regional Corporation. Like Todd Palin, my father worked his way up to a top position in his company. He was an operations manager, making a fortune compared to people in the rest of the country.

Whether Dad was away or home, every night my

mother somehow made us dinner and we sat down to eat like a family. She kept our house clean and did the laundry. She helped us with homework.

The homework arrangement wasn't easy for her because I didn't pay much attention in school. I felt like a prisoner. You know how when you're a kid in school you do a book report or a project and then you have to stand up in front of the class and talk about it? I hated that; I got nervous and fake-sick every time I had to do one.

If you didn't do your thing in front of the class, you got an automatic C. I took that C all day long.

They said I was restless, and it was true. I wanted to be anywhere but in that classroom.

They told Mom I had ADHD, attention-deficit/hyper-activity disorder. I was medicated with a healthy dose of Ritalin. It made for good housecleaning. I used to scrub the house, read books, and work on the house again. I wasn't good for much else though. I didn't talk and didn't eat. I felt terrible.

Before the Ritalin, everything was fine at home. When I was on it, my mom and Sadie were at the end of their ropes. My dad couldn't wait to get out of the house and back to work. He finally put his foot down when Ritalin screwed up my hockey game. My concentration was on the wrong thing. Unfolded towels on the bench. Trash on the floor. Not the crease, or the puck. It was all bad.

He says he's the one who took me off it. Mom says she

made the decision, that she just got fed up with Levi #2, so one day she threw away the meds.

That's as close as they get to agreeing on things.

I got off Ritalin but not off chew. All the hockey kids chewed tobacco. Dom's dad started me, without meaning to. He chewed Red Man. He always had these big old cheeks. Dom and I always wanted it because our dads were doing it. One time when I was ten and we were out fishing, Dom's dad and my dad were chewing, and so were Uncle Robbie and Uncle Mike.

I asked for some as usual, knowing the answer.

Uncle Mike said, Okay.

My dad said, What?

Let them do it. They'll be all right.

Mike smiled as he put a big old thing of Red Man in our cheeks.

To this day I keep at it and so does Dom.

Dad still chews, like almost every other Alaskan man. Sportsmen at least. I was a teen when one day I won't soon forget he picked me up from hockey and a Coke can was in the truck console. I was superthirsty and he was driving and not paying attention. I grabbed that damn thing and I started drinking. I got about a gulp into it and I realized it wasn't Coke.

I was sick. Oh, God, was I sick. He just loved it. He was choking with laughter.

My hockey playing got back to normal now that I, chewing away, was Ritalin-free and raring to go.

My dad came to every game he could. When working, he flew down from the Slope, then went right back.

I don't think Mom ever missed a match, unless she was barely out of the operating room.

I have this memory from when I was twelve. She was in the hospital and there was a big game.

She had to go.

No, the doc said, you can't.

What if, she bargained, I come back here after the game.

I made sure we won that one.

That night I realized my father was right, that I did have the skill to control the play. Could hockey be something I could do after high school? I wondered. Or in college? Maybe I'd get scouted like Dad did for football when he was in high school. Who knows, I said to myself as I swooped across the blue line, skating circles around other players, maybe I'll play pro.

Beyond Alaska.

That same year, Uncle Robbie, my mom's brother, and Grandpa Tim took me with them as they went up Little Willow Creek in an airboat, to then drift our way back down, hunting along the way. I was one happy kid, going on an adventure with Grandpa Tim, Uncle Robbie, and his dog. Ten days before, my dad had bought me a brand-new custom-made rifle. A .300 short mag. I sighted it in and it was good to go. I was so excited and remember thinking, I can't wait!

This was the same river system where gold had been discovered in 1906. We would not be as fortunate.

Grandpa Tim Zimbrich became my mom's stepdad when he married my grandmother Myrna. He taught me how to run an airboat when I was nine. I'd sit up on the high seat in front of the loud power of a plane engine taller than me, steering all by myself. Over logs I'd go, driving through drifts of brush.

That prop could have loped off my arm before I knew it. I'm not sure I'd let Tripp sit where I did, at that age, but it was as fun as hell.

Grandpa Tim and I had been out clamming half that spring, on ebb tides, the big ones. He had first taken me when I was five. He had his own small spade, and he got me an even smaller one. I had learned how to watch for bubbles in the sand when the tide was low, then dig like I was Mike Mulligan's steam shovel. I enjoyed taking them out of the sand and throwing them in a bucket, and I loved how I could see for great distances on the clam flats, gathering with no concern about who or what might be sneaking up on me.

The trip I took with Grandpa Tim and Uncle Robbie started off great. We were out there hunting for moose. We took turns running the airboat up the Little Willow. Uncle Robbie's dog, Ice, was with us, and we trailed our little jonboat behind the airboat and stopped at the site where we planned to spend the night. We unpacked our camping gear and set up a tent.

We piled back into the airboat with the jonboat still tied to the stern and took off for the headwaters of the Little Willow. Grandpa Tim was driving. He was going to drop us off once we'd gone as far as we could in the airboat. Then he'd motor down to our camp.

Uncle Robbie and I untied the jonboat and put our hunting stuff in it and got in. So did Ice.

Grandpa Tim turned around and went downstream, toward camp. We would end up there, too—after getting a moose along the way. I hoped.

We floated downstream in the jonboat, looking for a big moose. A sixty-four-inch spread of antlers is a big rack. If we broke sixty-five, we'd be doing really good. If we hit seventy, we'd have a monster.

Bull moose aren't mean. Cows can be if they have a calf. If you walk next to that baby or even close to it, that mom's coming. The bulls are pretty laid-back, and plenty ugly, but they do make damn good cheeseburgers, better than beef. Their ground meat has more flavor; it's juicy with a tangy hint of game.

We drifted along on the Little Willow. When the land looked ripe for moose or if we saw tracks coming to the water's edge, we'd pull the boat up onshore, and get out.

It was rough going along those banks. I stayed with the jonboat as Uncle Robbie moved in on the land a dozen paces and sat down to do a moose call. A moose will make a loud, guttural *E-r-r-r-a-a-a-h*, followed sometimes with a low whine. If Uncle Robbie grunts back, the moose'll reckon it's a bull and will want to fight, to challenge him, thinking that Robbie wants the bull's space and his lady.

Uncle Robbie had gotten back in the boat and I was daydreaming with my eyes closed as my uncle, Ice, and I went around an inside turn of the river, close to the edge. A sweeper was on the curve of the bank: right in front of us, a fallen tree was damming the water. Water ripped upstream behind the tree and created a gyre, spinning the Little Willow like a drain in a sink might do.

Now my eyes were wide-open. The whirlpool was ten yards wide.

I felt it coming. So did the dog, who hunkered down on the bottom, getting low. The water sucked us in.

We started to spin and lose control of the boat. We were swirling, getting dragged into it.

Uncle Robbie yelled, Jump! Jump!

The three of us, Robbie, Ice, and me, leapt out just in time, because as we bailed, the boat went under. We lost everything. My brand-new gun, the outboard, the boat— an easy ten grand counting binoculars and all kinds of shit. Uncle Robbie's new rifle was gone, too.

It was that quick. In seconds, we went from sitting in a boat to treading ice-cold water. I wasn't wearing a life jacket and am not the best paddler, but there I was, in the drink, splashing around. I was kicking, doing everything I could to get free of the swirl. I swam like a champ that day, almost as well as the dog. I made it out and crawled up the bank. The dog was there, watching Uncle Robbie until he climbed up, too.

There was nobody around. Nothing around.

It was forty degrees, and we were soaking wet. We could do nothing except sit and wait for Grandpa Tim to realize something was wrong and get into the airboat and come up the creek to look for us.

The sun went down, and no Grandpa Tim. Uncle Robbie and I finally decided we couldn't just sit out there any longer. Once it got dark, we knew he wasn't coming, and we had to get ourselves back or freeze.

We were ten miles from our camp, and off the creek was swamp after swamp.

We decided to risk swimming some to get back quicker. It was a dangerous idea, and I thought I was going to die in that water.

At about two miles down the creek Uncle Robbie saw an old, falling-down cabin on the other side. He remembered seeing a canoe there once and hoped it would still be there. He crossed to the other side to see if he could find it.

I climbed out, realized I could no longer feel my feet. I wanted to take off my boots but wasn't so hypothermic that my brain had gone wacky. I knew I mustn't unlace my shoes.

As Uncle Robbie waded in the water, he ordered his dog to stick by me, and I was glad to have him.

Alaskans have a connection to their dogs. They are bred to pull sleds and to hunt. That's their purpose. None of this cuddly stuff. You love your dogs, but if one isn't a good hunter, you pass him along. That sounds cold to people in the lower forty-eight. We feed them well. We provide good shelter. And they can't wait to get to work, pulling sleds, hunting in the woods.

It's what the dogs of Alaska do.

Ice sat by my leg. There's no way he'd do anything else when that's what Uncle Robbie had told him to do. If I moved a foot, so did Ice.

Ice and I wrapped ourselves around each other and waited to hear the sounds of a canoe in the water.

I was beginning to doze off when I heard Uncle Robbie yell out that there was no canoe, and no one was in the cabin.

He was whipped from crossing and even more frozen. Ice and I followed him from our bank, as he was too beat to cross over and we couldn't see a good spot. That was as scared as I've ever been, including when years later, Sarah would come after me. Uncle Robbie would call out every ten seconds or so to keep me going. The only thing keeping me on track was having Ice with me. He licked my hand and kept me calm.

Every time I was about to give up, tears streaming down my face, the dog would nudge me on.

A couple of hours and a million licks later, Uncle Robbie came upon a different canoe and paddled it over.

Ice waited for me to fall in over the gunwale, then he jumped in himself.

Uncle Robbie found a reserve of strength and rowed us back to camp. It was midnight, cold and pitch-black.

There was Grandpa in the big old tent, all warm. Well, where were you? he asked.

Where the fuck do you think we were? Uncle Robbie was so mad he was whispering, or he was just too exhausted to speak louder. I can see you leaving me out there, he said, but were you going to leave him?

Me. His grandson. Stepgrandson.

I couldn't stop shaking; I couldn't think. Uncle Robbie and Grandpa Tim stripped me down. I don't remember a whole lot. What I do know is that Ice kept me alive that day and night. He had never paid that much attention to me before, but after that night I feel like we formed a bond that lasted until the day he died.

I still see Grandpa Tim a couple of times a year, but my heart's not in it. He and I quit spending time together once my grandmother Myrna died, which was about the same time as the disaster on the Little Willow. I know I should forgive him; but I can't. Not completely.

He never came up the river for us.

As for my father, all he cared about was the damn gun sitting at the bottom of the Little Willow. He didn't process the whole deal till Robbie sat him down and told him the story. Even then he still wanted that gun back.

I'm going to kick Tim's ass, he said, spitting. After I kick yours for losing that gun.

My father, a scuba diver, decided he was going back to our spot on the creek and pull up those damn guns. Robbie went with him to point out the spot.

On his first dive, he came across a dead body pinned to the bottom. He surfaced and called 911. Half the state's law enforcement showed up. My dad transported them upstream in the airboat. Choppers, motorboats, dive team. Lights and sirens. It was a huge deal, reported in all the papers. Paramedics were there as the body was brought up from the deep, huge hole where it had been stuck.

It turned out to be a sex doll with flowing blond hair.

Dad never mentioned my gun again.

4

Me and My Babe

In 2005, I started high school, which only meant one thing to me: it was time to play hockey with the big boys.

I spent my first three weeks at Wasilla High acting like an asshole. I hooked up with older hockey buddies and I started puffing out my chest, strutting the corridors, and scaring the kids that everyone picked on. It gets me sick to think about what a jerk I was. I got in a fight my first week and had minor scrapes in weeks two and three. The school administration and the teachers were not impressed. I was too good at playing the hockey bad boy, and in short order, it was decided that I ought to go elsewhere.

I knew that homeschooled kids were allowed to play for Wasilla High, so I hatched a plan. I started working on Mom. The right thing to do, I told her, trying to keep the excitement out of my voice, is for you to homeschool me. I kept at it, pleading. She knew I hadn't been happy. She had had to deal with the bad parent-teacher conferences. Too many times she had been told that her son was disinterested and uninvolved and a discipline problem.

So Mom agreed to take on my schooling. Alaska has no regulations about homeschooling, no tests. Nothing. It's legal truancy. A parent in Alaska who decided to homeschool a kid had no forms to fill out. My state had no way to even know how many kids were being homeschooled. I didn't have to learn any particular thing for a certain number of hours or take any tests. The idea was to give moms and dads the freedom to teach whatever they wanted, or not. It should have been called no-schooling. It got pretty loose for some kids, who just hung out at home, loafing.

Mom didn't go that route. She actually made me work, and I could be around for her if she was having a bad day or week. I would go with her to her doctor's appointments.

I could be around for her like she was for me.

It was perfect.

I recall watching the other kids going to school thinking, I can't believe this. No more school, no more books or teachers' dirty looks. Especially those damn frowns.

As a homeschooled freshman, I played varsity on the Wasilla High hockey team and was Track Palin's teammate. Track, an old pal, was a sophomore. I slipped on a Wasilla Warriors wristband, and wore it for years after, as I outscored him—me, number 15, the freshman. I wasn't racking up more goals than just Track; I was first or second in points out of everybody. Almost first. I was always one of the top two or three players. For a time, I was the best. I played offense. Center and right wing.

Off the ice, I tagged along with the team's seniors. So did Track. We played with them on the ice; why not in town? Brothers-in-arms. One time my hockey pals Herbie and Dane and I were in Anchorage for a game. We pulled out our air guns on this downtown street—remember this was Anchorage, not Chicago or Atlanta—and were shooting at signs in front of a bank. Someone was watching on the bank's surveillance camera, and the police rolled up with guns drawn. They thought we were bank robbers. Once they saw we were just dopey kids, they let us go back to Wasilla.

I laugh at it now, but they scared the shit out of me. I never did anything like that again. Well, maybe once. Or twice. Like the time a Fish and Game cop pulled his weapon on me because I was fishing illegally. I had on the end of my line a rig that was over-the-top. It was a treble, or snag, hook. We called them white flies. Seriously bad. Added to that, I was salmon fishing in Moose Creek, a closed river. I could have gotten $5,000 in tickets, and possibly jail time, but I was lucky. I got a slap on the wrist and a $340 warning. The officer seized my fishing poles and all my fishing gear. I can still hear him explaining the shit I'd gotten myself into.

You know I can take your truck right now? he said.

Really? I wasn't being a smart-ass; I just couldn't believe it.

Yeah, and you don't get it back.

Government regulation of the great outdoors is a big deal in Alaska.

I learned quick, after these two experiences with guns pointed at me, that breaking the law wasn't the way to go.

From then on, I stayed at home when the boys were going to raise hell—like the time Track was sixteen and some friends, three seniors, got caught slashing school-bus tires. The Anchorage paper told the story.

Four high school students were arrested Monday on charges stemming from vandalism last week that disabled a school bus fleet, closing core-area schools for a day in the Matanuska-Susitna Borough School District, according to the Alaska State Troopers. Three boys—a 16-year-old and two 17-year-olds—were taken to the Mat-Su Youth Facility after their 10:30 a.m. arrests at their homes. The fourth, Deryck Harris, 18, was arrested at 2:51 p.m. at home and jailed at the Mat-Su Pre-Trial Facility.

The paper couldn't name the younger boys, but the gossip around town was that Track was one of them. There's no proof of that, so I don't know. The buses couldn't roll so the schools locked their doors. Everyone had a holiday but the parents and teachers weren't amused. Later on, when the Palins and the Johnstons weren't on good terms, Track, who was never charged, tried to say I was one of the guys. It was weird, his going back to that particular incident. Why did he do that? Who the hell knows. I never asked him, didn't really care. We both knew it was total bullshit. We both knew the truth.

The guys also got caught with fake IDs, and, again, the talk was that Track snuck under the wire on that one, too. I wouldn't have minded a fake ID, but it wasn't hard to find beer in Wasilla anyway. I was more interested in keeping my head down focusing on hockey—though I was also starting to notice a certain other Palin kid.

Track and I were hockey jocks. We were popular. Track was good-looking and well built, with a reputation the girls liked. The suggestion that he was a delinquent, true or false, added to that image.

Even though there were plenty of older kids, we were starters. Track was a big hitter and an intimidator; when he was on the ice, the other team learned to keep their heads up. I got put on the first line. I was a more of a finesse player, the one who made the goals. I was known to have a good backhand, and I could place my snap shot anywhere I wanted. The two good seniors on my line set me up to score and made me look better.

————

I wore a few different jerseys, not just the Wasilla's Indian with the feathered headdress, as I practiced and played with development or comp teams. Track did, too. In 2006, he and I found ourselves on different teams in different leagues when we both ended up in Fairbanks for a state tournament. My dad drove me up there and stayed for several days, making sure I did a good job.

Bonehead, he yelled at me when I missed a shot. You had a goddamn open net!

I wasn't worried about what my old man said. I had eyes, ears, and everything else aimed at a different target—Bristol Palin.

I'd seen her in the grocery store in Wasilla the day before the game. Track's sister, five months younger than me, was no longer a kid. She had on a soft-pink turtleneck sweater. Hot.

I walked right up to her. Just 'cause. 'Cause I couldn't keep away.

Are you coming to the games in Fairbanks? To see Track?

Are you playing? she asked. Her doe eyes looked right into me.

In that moment I swore I'd never shoot another deer.

She told me she'd try to come to the game, but didn't think she could get her mom to drive her. I wasn't hopeful either. In the past eight years, I'd only seen her mom at three, four games at most.

Not like my mom or my friends' moms.

The next night on the ice, I was running our conversation through my mind when I looked up and there she was. Bristol, her eyes fixed on me. As I headed for the bench during a line change, something electric happened over the heads of my teammates.

Lightning-bolt love.

It's lucky the ice didn't melt.

My dad and I were staying in a motel. The second night I asked him if I could borrow his truck to drive Bristol to the movies. I was fifteen and didn't have a license.

No!

Aw, Dad, are you sure? Please.

No!

Her body drove me crazy. All those curves and everything. It still does.

Before we all left Fairbanks, Bristol suggested that I come over after school the next day. I remember the dizzy feeling I felt when she opened the door for me and I walked in. The house was like a cavern. I thought my voice would cause an echo. Shaq would have found it comfy. Windows filled the back wall, that overlooked Lake Lucille. There were crummier houses along the waterfront, even a house or two down from the Palins' place, but it was and is a beautiful setting.

The first time I arrived when Bristol wasn't yet home, her mom answered the door.

You betcha, she said, smiling, when I asked if I could come in out of the snow to wait.

Back when I was a twelve-year-old playing hockey with Track Palin, I'd called her "Mayor Palin." Now, when I did, she waggled her finger.

Levi, you don't have to call me Mayor.

How about Mrs. Palin?

She smiled and shook her head. Sarah, she said.

When I entered the Palin home on those high school afternoons, she would be in her favorite spot in the living room, on the leather sofa. She always had on a sweat shirt and PJ bottoms with silly little characters. She'd pat the cushion next to her for me to join her.

Sitting there, Sarah and I would talk about the kids, her clothes, and her Wasilla pals, who met for lattes at Kaladi Brothers Coffee near Chimo Guns. She'd tell me about the home shows she followed on TV, and the soaps.

Sarah kept me from getting bored, waiting for Bristol.

When she walked in the door, Sarah would disappear into her bedroom for the rest of the day and my babe and I were together.

It was comfortable to fall into homemaking mode. It felt so easy and cozy with her, like slipping on my camo slippers. She acted the role of parent with her younger siblings: Willow her sister, who was a damn independent eleven-year-old, and her littlest sister Piper, a spunky kindergartner. We'd all go out to the basket outside and shoot hoops. Except Bristol. She'd watch, then go and start dinner, and I'd come in before the kids and help out. We'd all watch movies afterward. Make popcorn. It felt like home.

I knew her brother, and her sisters. Bristol said she wanted me to get to know her dad. The first time I went snow machining with him, he surprised me. At home he is like a shadow. Always in the garage, doing something. Away from home, Todd was a totally different guy. He opened up and we had fun together. Todd and I got home one night and he walked back into his house, past Sarah, who was on her way to her bedroom with her typical dinner, a Diet Coke and chips. They didn't say a word to each other, yet Todd's face darkened. He went back to his usual grumpy self and headed for his hidey-hole, the garage, where he could be alone. He was a hardworking guy who was employed by BP on the Slope for years and whose sweethearts, now that he'd eased off the job, were the beloved snow machines he tinkered with constantly. I watched him rebuild one of them, an Arctic Cat. He'd pick up a tool, then place it carefully back where it belonged before reaching for another.

When he and I went out to his cabin, we got along great as long as Sarah was far away.

———

For the most part, Sarah was as distant as Todd. She gave out hugs and handshakes to the public, but in private, she didn't reach out to her kids. If she was in one of her hyperjoyful moods, then she might grab one of them as they went by. Otherwise, she left them alone.

If they wanted something, she'd give in, always. It wasn't important to her to get her own way about unimportant stuff—things she wasn't all that interested in.

Most days, by the time Bristol and Willow got home, Sarah was out of sight. She'd be in her first-floor, cavernlike bedroom with its big walk-in closet—that might have been a huge master bedroom, but it was all hers, not Todd's, although he kept his clothes in there. He spent his time in his workshop in the garage, with overnights in the living room. Still dressed.

Track hung out with his own friends, not with his dad, and not with me. Even though he came over to my house when we were kids and we'd been close on the rink—and here I was now in his house—I didn't see him much. No one knew where he was and nobody asked. I sure didn't. I was into Bristol.

I was spending more time with her family than she did.

The word *family* meant something different in their blocky, chestnut-colored house than it did in my little, gray one. When I was growing up, every night my parents, my sister, Sadie, and I sat down—just the three of us when Dad was on the Slope—for an evening meal. The Palins never did; there wasn't a connection like we Johnstons had.

They ate whenever they wanted, whatever they wanted, and wherever they wanted. The kids and adults didn't cross paths. Their dining table had shit all over it. It was a junk catchall with Piper's toys and books piled high, with sweaters hanging off the backs of the chairs. I never saw all of them in the dining area at the same time, and never did they say grace together before a meal.

I'm not religious, but I do pray when I'm hunting. I pray nobody gets eaten. I don't think the Palin group prayed at all. They went to church on Christmas Eve with Sarah's parents, the Heaths. That was, as far as I knew, the only time that they did.

Todd spent his days and nights in the garage working on his sleds and neatening up his tools and workbench.

Sarah and her two CrackBerrys—one business; one personal—stayed in the bedroom with its flat-screen TV.

Money would appear on the black kitchen counter for someone to buy food.

As I headed into sophomore year, Mom decided that there would be no more homeschooling. After a year of that freedom for me, Mom thought I needed to be with other kids. She said socialization was important.

I was on the road as well, playing hockey. Whenever I was not, Bristol and I were together.

Bristol started at Wasilla High, while I wound up at Burchell. It was a smaller, more personal high school, and my mom felt it would be a better fit for me. I could still play hockey at Wasilla High; Burchell didn't have a team.

Being a real student meant having to show up at class, at least on Wednesdays and Fridays, which were practice and game days. This required serious discipline on my part. I had missed most days in the past, even in grade school. My parents didn't usually know. I'd go home and erase the answering machine. Whenever my dad did catch me, he'd freak out.

Now, he wanted me to be eligible to play. I had to keep a 2.0 grade point average. I was with him on that. I don't think I learned a lot during the year I was homeschooled, but by sophomore year I was older, a little wiser, and better motivated. I found myself back in a classroom, but this time, instead of daydreaming, I paid attention. It was the first time I'd ever been involved with what was going on in school. Before that I was just getting by. I was like a C and D kid.

My grades began to improve. I began getting B's along with the C's.

By the end of my sophomore year in the spring, I would be chosen for a 2007 U.S. Select Team. I got to travel to the lower forty-eight to play in Olympic rinks in Lake Placid and Portland, Oregon.

I ended up in the Nationals and I loved it.

I was as excited as Sarah was at the start-up for her campaign. It was the fall of 2006 and she wanted to be governor. She held a couple of meetings with campaign people at the house, but Bristol and I were always upstairs, in our own world.

Sarah was appearing here and there, in Anchorage, Fairbanks, Valdez. Her family-values rap meant she needed to drag her kids along now and then. Todd, the spouse, too. Willow, already the rebel at age twelve, opted out. The private Bristol hated it but gave in. Piper, the free spirit, was loving it. She could have been her mom's campaign manager; she was her most enthusiastic supporter.

On November 7, 2006, Sarah won the race by a landslide. I got the news on the phone from a giggling Bristol. Sarah killed her opponent, Bristol said. It's terrible, she told me, then giggled some more.

Sarah took office on December 4, 2006, and announced to her family that they would all be moving to the governor's mansion in Juneau.

5

Her Honor the Governor

You can't drive directly to Juneau from Wasilla. You have to go eight hundred miles through Canada's Yukon Territory, then swing back into the United States, toward the coast at Haines. Then you put your car on the ferry from Haines to Juneau.

It takes about twenty hours to make that trip. The alternative is to fly.

I have never been there. I didn't know any Wasillian who had, besides the Palins, and even they would keep as far away as possible when Sarah was governor.

It was hard on Bristol, expecting her to become a second-semester sophomore at Juneau-Douglas High School and leave me and Wasilla behind. Why did she have to go just because her mom decided to be governor?

Todd became the First Dude, but he didn't change much. He was most happy in his garage, where we would still meet up and share a beer. It's where he hid his brew.

Todd supported Sarah, although he believed that Alaska should secede from the Union, and he didn't see much use for government. That was a popular sentiment. In Alaska, each citizen is entitled to a yearly stipend—a tiny percentage of the state's oil profits, usually a few thousand dollars. I didn't take my yearly Alaska Permanent Fund money. I'm responsible for taking care of myself, not the government. Not unless I can't do it. The new arrivals in Wasilla always bellied up. They liked to think that Alaska wasn't really joined to the lower forty-eight, until they needed something like oil cleanup money or spring-flood housing assistance. Then they were delighted to get whatever federal funds they could get.

Regardless of his core politics and beliefs, Todd stood by Sarah and made it clear to all comers that any slight against her would be a score he would settle.

Sarah came to hate the isolation of Juneau as much as her daughters did and began keeping an office in Anchorage complete with a tanning bed like the one in her bedroom. Bristol and her sisters would also come back to Wasilla whenever Sarah did. Track spent his senior year with a family in Michigan, filling a slot on an AAA hockey team in Kalamazoo. I didn't see him much at all, but it was good that he was in a more stable environment. He was having some major anger issues on the ice.

For me it was all about the times that Bristol made it home. Even with the full Palin house, it felt like we were the only ones there. Willow was out with her friends, Piper off in bed, Todd in the garage with his snow machines, and

Sarah in her downstairs room. Those times with Bristol are some of my favorite memories.

We'd stay up all night talking about the future. My getting a job on the Slope, the two of us buying a house in the 'Silla. It all sounded good, though I still had my hockey dream.

In early spring of 2007, Track came home. His mom said he injured his shoulder playing hockey. The word around the streets of Wasilla—and there are only a few—was that he was kicked off the Michigan team and was forced to enlist in the military. Track wasn't the kind of kid who would choose to sign up. He went on active duty with the First Stryker Brigade Combat Team, based at Fort Wainwright in Fairbanks. In September of 2008, Track was deployed to the Middle East to serve in Iraq.

I didn't care about Bristol's wayward brother. Neither did she. We had other things on our minds. The snow had melted and we would leave the house to escape into the woods, my favorite place on earth. She was the sun of my life. We became secret camping lovers, scraping gnarly gnats off our lips before we kissed. We spent our days fishing, and I used up more energy undressing her with my eyes than I did tying on flies.

I love you, I'd started to say, and before I finished, she'd said the same thing to me.

The next day, Bristol told her mom we were in love.

No, said Sarah.

Yes!

You're just good friends, Sarah told her daughter, then walked away. She knew though; she knew we had a relationship.

That night, Sarah went out to a meeting. We were upstairs in Bristol's room when we heard Todd's diesel truck go down the driveway. So we decided to chance taking a shower together. We were in the middle of shampooing each other's hair when we heard the truck come back. I freaked! I was drying off my hair with one hand and hers with the other, as she pulled our clothes out of the pile on the floor.

I tried to make it downstairs before he got inside, but I was too slow.

We listened as Todd came in and opened the fridge, then I heard the creak of his recliner. When I stuck my cap on my head and strolled downstairs, I had to look like the most obvious perp in Wasilla. None of it mattered. Bristol's dad was asleep.

We were more careful when we took a bubble bath downstairs in Sarah's Jacuzzi. This time we made sure we knew where everyone was going and for how long. Still, my ears stayed perked like a bear's.

Bathing together in Sarah's sacred tub would have caused a stir.

It wasn't ever a problem when we were in Bristol's room.

We did whatever we wanted there, with its Jack-and-Jill bathroom shared with Willow—and ruled by Bristol.

A week later Bristol gave me a promise ring. It was silver. I hated gold, would never have worn it unless it was silver. She had engraved on the inside I LOVE YOU. BRISTOL.

I never got the promise-ring concept. If she was giving it to me, did that mean she was the one promising? Or was it that, as I slipped it on, I was hog-tied, not to look at another female? I had a feeling, since it was Bristol, I was the one with an obligation. Maybe I should have thought more about its being a one-sided deal. What the hell. I had eyes for no one but my babe.

Silver or gold, she knew I didn't like rings. They get caught in stuff when you're in the bush.

6

The Trickster

During the second week in August of 2007, and two days before sheep season opened, I left for a hunt in the Talkeetna Mountains. It was me, my cousin Dom, and Derek Larson. My father's pilot, Mike Meekin, took us where few pilots will go.

We flew out a few days early to do prep work—set up camp, scout out the area, find some sheep—so we could start hunting on the first official day of the season.

The three of us climbed the alpine ridges of the rugged terrain. It's different in Alaska than in Canada, where hunters can rent helicopters. A chopper delivers those guys to the top of the mountains. We Alaskans reach the bottom by fixed-wing plane and hike our way up.

You can only hunt a Dall sheep that is at least eight years old. So you look at the horns. From the base they've got to curl all the way around, and you have to count the rings. There must be at least eight. This means you spend hours sitting and watching. The sheep are clever and hide behind rocks. It takes patience and concentration; I love it.

We came up on a group of four rams. Only one was legal. I let Dom take it because it wasn't a big one. Dom shot and missed. Four hundred yards. I couldn't believe it. So we chased them. Then we got socked in with fog; we had to use GPS to find our camp. That's how it was for three more days. We had to stay in our little camp. Three whole days, doing nothing. The fog finally cleared, but the next day we had to leave.

I didn't get to hunt.

It was freezing up there, even in August. The weather was terrible. The fog was so thick I couldn't see the next mountain. At one point I pulled off my gloves, and the damned promise ring slipped off my finger. As I was looking all over the ground for the promise ring, I heard the cry of a raven. Ravens are all over Alaska. The raven is a trickster in Native Alaskan mythology. One was wheeling over my head, looking down at me with one eye, laughing. I was sure he had seen the glitter of the ring and scooped it up. Somewhere in Alaska there is a nest with a little silver trinket in it that says I LOVE YOU. BRISTOL.

It felt like a bad omen. Since that day, every damn action I've taken and the actions of everyone around me have had *bad* written all over them.

Seventeen years old and fucked.

The first wave of bad luck came when I was back from the lost-ring sheep hunt and Mom, always up for a happy celebration, had planned a big family cookout. Dad was nowhere to be seen. My mom was getting hot under the collar, although this was nothing new.

My father had been seeing the same woman on the side for years. My mother was self-reliant and didn't play the victim. I remember coming home from school when I was a kid and walking in on my parents' fights. I was young enough, maybe only five, that I didn't understand their words, but the message was clear.

Over and over, Mom would throw his shit out on the lawn.

Dad would leave, but he'd always come back two or three days later. From Lisa's. His mistress. I tried to ignore her existence.

The day after the sheep hunt, we were all out back on the patio and listening for Dad's truck. My mother had a hunch where he was. So she did a drive-by. Dad's truck was there, parked in Lisa's driveway. Mom pulled up and he ran toward the garage to make a getaway. She flipped out and ended up nose-to-nose with Lisa.

The situation was almost like one you see on TV, where both parties attack the police.

This was the beginning of twelve months of grief, the last year my parents would be together.

At the end of the summer of 2007, love was still in the air for Bristol and me. My family situation might be pretty bleak, but for the two of us, the days were long and filled with sunshine. Bristol had been in Wasilla her whole vacation. I was working with my dad on electrical jobs around town, and as I pulled wires, all I could think about was Bristol.

It would have been nice if Bristol had shared. Instead, I learned of her threat when Sarah, hands on her hips, asked me just what my plan was.

Plan? I said.

Where is it you think you and Bristol will go?

Huh?

Bristol had said we'd run away before she'd spend another semester in Juneau.

Sarah said Bristol was a pain and caused problems. Sarah didn't like it. Oh, really? It was Bristol, the housekeeper and nanny, who gave Todd and especially Sarah the freedom to do whatever the hell they wanted, as their oldest daughter took on what should have been their responsibilities.

Parenting is more than leaving fifty bucks on the kitchen counter.

They reached a compromise. Bristol would move to Anchorage, forty miles from Wasilla, to live with her aunt Heather, Sarah's older sister. Bristol would sign up at Anchorage's West High School for her junior year.

I was still attending Burchell and playing hockey with Wasilla High, and I spent time trucking between my home and Anchorage. Montgomery Gentry's "It's All Good" juiced me up along the way to see Bristol. Most of the time, Bristol came to me—through snow and sleet and, finally, the rain of springtime.

One weekday in March 2008, Bristol called me and said she was in Wasilla. She sounded as if she was being strangled.

What's wrong, babe? I asked her.

Can you come over right away?

Oh, Jesus, I was thinking. She's pregnant. I hadn't been concerned as nothing had happened in the two years we'd been together. Dumb.

I met her at her house. Sarah was in her own room; Todd was in his garage. Maybe. No one usually had any idea where Todd was. The kids were here and there, sometimes around, sometimes not. Bristol dragged me up the carpet of the L-shaped staircase, closed her bedroom door behind us.

I'd spent hours there holding her in my arms, running my fingers through her hair. I loved her hair. I loved every inch of her. I was about to make this statement with my hands when Bristol laid her hand over mine. It felt like a cold salmon.

I looked at her. Her face fell. I thought she might cry. I had no idea why.

Before I could say anything, it was out of her mouth.

My parents, she told me, are having another baby. She said the word *parents* with air quotes.

I never—and I mean never—saw Sarah and Todd touch

71

or kiss, other than for a photo op. They barely even talked to each other, and when they did, it was about practical stuff like who could watch the kids or who would pick them up from a friend's house. I had more conversations with the guy who bags my mom's groceries at the Carrs/Safeway than those two did with each other. *Hmhf.* I guess Sarah and Todd were intimate at some point after all. I didn't share this thought with Bristol.

The infant was due in two months.

Rumors and speculation that Bristol was going to have a baby had circulated for over a year. That tale had spread from the halls of Wasilla High, through town, and from one end of the state to the other. As I think about it now, I wonder if she had told friends what she said to me—that she was dying to have our baby—and they carried it a step further. The whispers started when, after Sarah had been sworn in as governor in December '06, Bristol left Wasilla and moved to Juneau for the second semester of her sophomore year. Then the word was that the family was saying that Bristol, who was MIA, had mono. For the record, Bristol never had mono, no one would have said she did—and she wasn't pregnant then. I kept telling her to ignore all this silliness, but she had trouble doing that. Once she even called Sarah at work, asking Sarah to do something to make the ugly rumors stop. Bristol was crying, upset.

Her mom's response: *Too bad.*

———

I wasn't doing such a good job paying attention to Bristol's mood myself, her negative reaction to her mom's pregnancy. Wow, I said. Your mom sure doesn't look pregnant.

When I think back on it, maybe she did, a little. She had started putting around her neck this scarf-y shit that hung down the front of her. She usually wore clothes that showed what she had. She was dressing a little different, with these looser outfits. When I'd told her how nice she looked, she had thrown her arms around me.

She definitely did a good job hiding her baby bump. I guess I can understand why she was keeping it a secret. She had to always be watching her back. I guess she expected her political enemies to claim she couldn't do her job with a newborn in tow.

So, long jackets and scarves.

Hiding it from the public is one thing, but from her family?

Both Bristol and Willow had noticed that their mom was putting on weight. Are you calling me fat? she'd said to Bristol.

Then Willow was snooping around and found a Clearblue pregnancy stick in one of her mom's drawers. It was positive. Bristol's next words brought me back to attention.

I'm the one, Bristol said, who should be having a baby. Not Sarah.

The Palin kids call their parents Todd and Sarah when things are tense.

Bristol looked at me. Let's get pregnant.

I'm not ready, I remember thinking. I'm just a kid.

I stopped stroking her hair.

Sarah supposedly considered aborting her baby; after all, no one knew she was pregnant. Her choice, she would say in speeches, was to carry little Trig full term. She would later write in her book, *Going Rogue*:

> *I sighed and stared at the ceiling.* These are really less-than-ideal circumstances. . . . *And for a split second it hit me:* I'm out of town. No one knows I'm pregnant. No one would ever have to know.

It was odd that Sarah wanted the country to be pro-life, yet she herself exercised her right to consider options. Isn't her right to make that choice exactly what pro-lifers want to get rid of?

I didn't like abortion—who does? At the same time, I wasn't the one who should be telling someone else what to do. I didn't think I should control the rest of the world. Sarah did, but her own rules didn't apply to her.

I found out from Bristol that the child would probably be a Down's baby. Sarah had waited to tell anyone about the pregnancy until the seventh month, and maybe a month later, right before the baby arrived four weeks early, she

told them about the Down's. She herself had known for a
few months.

Trig was born April 18, 2008.

I got a phone call way early that morning when it was
still dark. It was Bristol, who I had just left a few hours
before. I knew Sarah was flying home from Texas, but that
was all. I don't think Bristol or anyone else in the family
knew Sarah might be getting ready to deliver the baby.

Then she called home from Anchorage as soon as
she got to her car in the airport parking lot, and Bristol
called me.

Mom thinks she might be about to go into labor, Bristol said into my ear. We're meeting her at the hospital.

Sarah had been telling Bristol during the past month
that her water was leaking once or twice a day, in drops.
When she left for the lower forty-eight, though, her baby
wasn't due for another five weeks. I had told Bristol it was
nuts for her mom to be traveling here and there, giving
speeches. I sure as hell wouldn't have let Bristol do that.
Now Sarah was telling Bristol that the drops were pretty
much constant. Sarah had felt she had plenty of time to get
back to Wasilla. She wanted to be home rather than deliver
in Texas so that her new son could be a true-blue Alaska
boy. She wanted this child, possibly a Down's baby, to be
delivered by her doc, who knew the deal, in our new medical center in Wasilla. If there were complications, she didn't
want to end up stuck in Texas.

I was only partially awake, and said to Bristol, Okay. I'll come down later, after I get a little more sleep.

I arrived just minutes after the birth. Bristol was in her mom's delivery room when I walked in. Todd was there, too.

So was Trig. My heart went out to the delicate child. I picked him up, cuddled him. Something stirred deep within me. It was like the instinct that surfaced whenever my sister, Sadie, needed her big brother's protection. Trig's face had the signs of Down's. He didn't have rounded cheeks, and his eyes had that slant. His tongue seemed big, too much for his mouth to handle. He needed care and I wanted to be sure he got it. I felt an adult emotion for the first time.

As I welcomed Trig into the world, I had no idea I'd be repeating this same display of affection for my own child just eight months later. Bristol, also unaware she was carrying our own tiny secret, took the newborn into her arms. Todd watched from the wings.

Between the flight and the delivery, Sarah was pale, whipped. There'd be help at home when she got there. A retired special-needs teacher had been lined up to care for the infant.

Sarah was back at work for only a couple of days before the old rumor, that Bristol had been pregnant all along, resurfaced. After Trig's arrival, people believed that Bristol, not Sarah, had given birth to Trig. I wondered who they thought the father might be. Oh.

As Sarah slipped into her old routine, back and forth to Anchorage, with an occasional trip to Juneau, the furor about Trig—was Bristol the real mommy?—continued. We pretty much ignored it; it was too crazy for words.

We had no idea right then how much more insane things would get. That May, two days before my eighteenth birthday, Bristol called me from her aunt's house in Anchorage. She said, Hey, I'm coming out. I miss you, babe. She was all kinds of excited.

It was a Thursday. I'd gone to all my classes and just walked in the door of our house, with my homework in my backpack. That past semester I had pulled a 3.8 GPA. I'd been thinking more and more about the connection between good grades and a possible future in hockey. It had dawned on me that the next year college scouts would need to see that I could deal with not just sports, but academics, too. I kept my nose buried in the books as much as possible, thinking I could actually get an athletic scholarship. I wanted to play junior hockey and try to get into the Western Hockey League and then go pro. I had already been looked at by a WHL team. By the time I was nineteen, I would have been good enough to play for them, or the University of Alaska. UA told me I just needed the grades.

I'd gotten them.

My tibia was fractured, but despite that, by the season's last game I was playing the best hockey of my life. I was thinking of talking to Bristol about all this when it hit me.

Are you pregnant? I asked her over the phone.

No.

Are you lying?

No, she shot back. I'm not fucking lying.

Fine, I told her. But I knew.

She hadn't stopped talking about having a baby since her brother Trig had arrived two weeks before. Earlier than that, actually. Before her mom had even announced her own pregnancy. When she started talking about it, I asked her about birth control, but she assured me that everything was safe. I only half believed her. I have to admit that the thought of me making a little one always lit me up. With Bristol, who I loved, I wasn't paying as much attention as I should have.

She showed up at my house, and then she pulled one of these Clearblue plastic pregnancy tests out of her purse. The word PREGNANT leaped out at me. I didn't know what to say or what to do. My heart just stopped.

She was crying and laughing and then we were hugging. It was what she wanted; it had happened. I had been too dumb to wrap it up with care. We'd been lucky since freshman year, and a part of me thought that maybe I was shooting blanks. She and I had talked about birth control pills, and she had gone to the doc. I'd seen the case of pills in her bathroom, and I just assumed she was taking them.

I know I sound idiotic here, but I'm not the first guy to act so clueless. I'm also not the first to get caught by my carelessness.

The whole situation reminded me of a lesson I thought

I'd learned when I was a kid. That was when I had had a one-on-one with a goat. My dad, uncle, and cousin Dom and I went hunting for mountain goats. Dad had gotten himself a decent goat the first day and he was satisfied. Dom and I were there to help carry the packs and to deer hunt on the side.

Dom and I decided to drop down on the other side of a ridge, to tree level, where we might see deer. My father ambled behind, keeping an eye on us, just in case.

The deer were forgotten when we came across a huge mountain goat, heading down the far side of a drainage. The billy goat didn't see me. I was above and off to the side. I dropped everything and took off after him, slipping on stones as I wound around boulders, heading off the goat. I was playing around. I wanted to see how close I could get.

I knew my dad was sitting above with his gun, ready to shoot the goat if it started threatening me. I moved in, waiting for the goat to come down on the far side.

The goat then popped up where I didn't expect him. All of a sudden, he was a just a couple of truck lengths away. I could see his long hairs. Because I had no gun, it was almost scarier than a bear.

I pictured my dad, way up above, backing me up. I hoped.

That big, old goat dropped his head down on his deep chest and aimed his black horns right at me.

Oh, God, I remember thinking. I'm gonna be gored by a fucking goat.

Lucky for me, he lifted up his head, took another look, and decided I was boring. He took off. There was a lesson to be learned there, though.

Never turn a serious situation into a game.

I thought about that as Bristol and I stood hugging. A baby? I couldn't believe it. Oh, shit. I was numb, but excited, too. I didn't realize it was going to change my whole life. I didn't realize anything at all.

We went upstairs and told my mom that Bristol was expecting. My dear mother started talking about having a little grandbaby. She put her arms around Bristol and patted her tummy—just a little more rounded than usual. Bristol let out with her great laugh. I loved seeing them like this together, the two women who meant so much to me.

My mom asked Bristol, Have you told your parents?

No, and I'm not going to, said Bristol, hands on her hips. My mom didn't tell me she was pregnant, did she? Why should I tell her?

I could kind of understand where Bristol was coming from. Sarah only told her family that she was expecting just before the media broke the story to the whole world.

A sharp-eyed Willow—the Palin pregnancy police—had been eyeing Bristol, even asking her if she was pregnant. Bristol denied it; at that point she still didn't know. Willow didn't buy into that. She began searching Bristol's room. Two days after Bristol had told me the news, ever-snooping Willow found what she was looking for. In her older sister's purse, there it was: that positive Clearblue thing. These Palin women must have bought those tests in bulk.

Just as she had threatened her mom if she didn't come clean with the family, Willow now warned us that she would tell Sarah and Todd unless we manned up and told them ourselves. Immediately.

I'll be damned, Bristol said to me, if I'm going to tell Sarah!

I told her it had to be us who faced the music and broke the news to Sarah and Todd, not Willow.

Bristol had to cave in the end.

Bristol had initially told only her cousin Lauden, Aunt Heather's daughter, about the pregnancy. It was Sammy Becker though, an old Wasilla friend, who Bristol recruited for moral support. The three of us headed for the Palin house. It was the day after I turned eighteen. I was on my way to nineteen, and fatherhood.

When we got there, Sarah was in her room. I could hear her treadmill. I pictured her in her vest deal with the weights.

Bristol texted her, asking her to come out to talk. The treadmill motor died.

The three of us sat and waited. We listened to the Alaska Railroad train go by. The Palin house is like one hundred yards from the track. It feels like it's running through the living room when you first hear it.

The train's crossing whistle blew. I was used to the blast

and so was Bristol. Sammy jumped. I realized a second later Sammy's reaction hadn't been to the train whistle.

Sarah had come out of her room and was heading toward us.

She was wearing her usual sweatshirt and printed jammies bottoms. That day it was polar bears. The cleaning lady wasn't around. As far as I could see, neither were Todd or the other kids. Bristol and I inched a little farther forward on the sofa. I realized that I'd been holding my breath and forced myself to exhale. The house always felt emotionally cold, and that day it was more glacial than ever. I felt like I was center ice, headed for the penalty box for a five-minute major before the game even began.

I wasn't ready to share our news with the Sarah who called me her best friend. Bristol was a wreck. Sammy kept throwing Bristol these looks. Come on. Get going. Say something. Then Sammy worked me, less encouraging and more insistent. It's time to let it out. Speak up.

Sarah took off her titanium Kawasaki glasses—$250 a pop—used her sweatshirt to clean them, and put them back on.

Finally Sammy gave up and blurted it out.

Levi and Bristol are going to have a baby.

Sarah broke out in laughter. You're kidding.

Mom. Bristol's voice sounded like Piper's. We are.

Silence. Then Sarah turned her head and drew a bead on me.

I don't believe it, she said. She shook her head. No.

She was staring so hard that I felt paralyzed. It was like getting too close to a bear. I had heard that Sarah Barracuda had a killer streak. Until that moment though, I never knew what people had been talking about.

Sarah kept a gun under her bed, but she had no idea how to load it, much less shoot it. She once pulled it out, shook some bullets out of their box, and asked me to show her what to do.

At this moment, I was happy I had opted out.

Sarah jumped up off the red sofa and went out to the garage. She returned with Todd in tow. It was just luck that he happened to be there. Todd the ghost. Except when his temper got inflamed. Like now.

Todd sat down in his recliner. That chair had been through hell. Sarah collapsed back on the couch, slipped off her eyeglasses, cleaned them again on her sweatshirt. She put them on, she looked at me. She turned her head when I caught her eye. If she was trying to send me a message, I wasn't getting it.

Todd, who had been watching Sarah first, and then me, was in that place where some quiet men go. Look out.

Do you think I'm going to support Bristol and your baby? His voice was loud. Suddenly he wasn't so quiet after all.

Well, no.

You need to quit school, get a job.

Sarah picked up. You guys are going to have to get married.

Maybe. After we graduate, I was thinking. Had been thinking.

This was the only time she mentioned marriage—until, that is, the McCain team would make it an issue.

There was no talk of abortion. Sarah would later say that she told Bristol it was her choice and her daughter made the right one. Frank Bailey in his book, *Blind Allegiance to Sarah Palin*, said Sarah told him the same thing. That's total fiction, although Sarah might be deluding herself or just doesn't know the truth. Bristol got pregnant on purpose. She had finally come clean, admitted to me that she hadn't been taking her birth control pills. We were having a baby, end of story. I wonder why Sarah felt the need to claim other options were considered.

It's an odd thing to say about your daughter if it isn't true.

Another odd comment was made a year later, when an interview of Bristol and Sarah was reported in *In Touch Weekly*. Sarah said she and her daughter believed they'd redeemed themselves by making the decision to keep the baby. Sarah made a decision? There was no considering any other options; Bristol had been *trying* to have a baby.

7

We're Pregnant

My sister and mom were invited over to the Palins' to check in with Todd and Sarah and to welcome Trig. Sadie, a camera bug, was snapping photos of everyone, and I shot one of her holding Trig, a smiling Sarah at her elbow. The Johnston and Palin adults went out together one night. Everyone seemed to be getting used to the idea that Bristol and I would be parents, too.

That's what we thought, at least, until Bristol got a call from Sarah a week later. Bristol and I had driven east to Rebirth Tattoo, over on the Wasilla-Palmer line. I was making up for losing the promise ring by having Bristol's name inked in the place where the ring should have been. It hurt like hell, but Bristol was loving the way her name looked wrapped around my finger in Gothic type. She was already talking about how much she was going to lick it and kiss it to death.

That's when her cell went off. I was looking anywhere but at my finger so I zoned in on Bristol's face. I watched it fall.

No, Sarah, she said. That won't be happening.

No. Levi and I want this baby. We are not giving it to you. Never.

I could hear her mother's voice. She was saying that she and Todd would be adopting our baby to avoid a scandal.

No. No. No. Bristol's forehead was a series of crinkly lines. No. Nope. I don't care. No.

I'm worried, Sarah said to Bristol, about you.

She'd already told her attorney, Thomas Van Flein, to draw up the papers.

Bristol flipped out. She was shaking, speechless. I caught the phone as it fell out of her hand.

Now I was doing the talking.

Look, Sarah, we appreciate the offer and know you care but . . .

No matter what I said or how strongly, Sarah kept on message.

It'll be okay, I told her. No, I don't care if people know, and neither does Bristol. In fact, she likes to tell people that she's—

Again she cut me off, to say the same damn thing. That's how she won arguments. She never gave in. Exhaustion would overtake the opponent and she'd be the victor.

Sarah, I—

Sarah, I need to end this conversation . . . nothing more to discuss—

After about ten tries, I knew it was useless.

I had to hang up on her.

Sarah had told Bristol she wanted to be the mom to my child, but it wasn't going to be that way. My babe and I would have this baby and raise it together. It was ironic that Sarah offered to be a mother to another child considering that she basically ignored the ones she already had.

I believed the choice to have a child included the obligation to be parents to that child. In Wasilla, we might have been the pioneers of this concept. So many pregnant teens were in the high school the next year that they opened a nursery. It was wall-to-wall packed with babies. Maybe Bristol was a role model—for teen pregnancy.

I don't support this, my father told me, when I announced I was dropping out of school. I want you to get your diploma; stay in school. Mom and I can help you work this out. His words echoed the expression I'd seen on my mother's face, if only for a second, when we told her Bristol was pregnant.

I respected my father's opinion but I needed to earn money, not take from them. Todd had made that clear, though I'd already figured it out for myself. I decided to look for a good-paying spot on the North Slope. I had tons of references, along with hours working with my father for DG Smith Builders in Wasilla. I sent in an apprentice electrician's application to Dad's company, the Arctic Slope Regional Corporation. ASRC knew who I was with Sarah being governor—and my pop oversaw all ASRC construction on the North Slope. He told me to say I had my GED. The job wouldn't open until August or September. By then, he said, you'll have the GED. Bristol liked this idea, and we started to plan our lives around it. I hung up my skates. It was time to be a working man. I did, though, continue to wear my Wasilla High wristband, just to remember those times.

That July, Sarah was going to speak at a Wynonna Judd concert in Anchorage, at the Elmendorf Air Force Base. She reached out and invited my mom and sister to join her, along with a couple of Palin relatives. Sarah's staff was there to hold and rock a three-month-old Trig.

I told Sarah how nice that was of her. Sadie had a ball, and Mom acted as if she did. Dad had finally moved out. My father, even though he'd been seeing Lisa on and off for years, waited until Sadie and I were grown to leave my mom; I think he waited because his own father did not.

I was working residential construction jobs in Wasilla, mostly as an electrician's helper, and waiting to hear from ASRC.

The Palins also had some waiting going on. Big-time. First Rudy Giuliani said he could imagine Alaska governor Sarah Palin as his running mate. Then, once he was out of the race, the chitchat throughout the country—on TV, in the press, and all over the Internet—was that John McCain was eyeing her to fill the VP slot if he was nominated.

Sarah flitted around the house in one of her hyperjoy-ful states. She was ecstatic.

Todd, not so much. She might have been a contender for national office, but he was doing what he always did. He was getting ready for the Iron Dog race. Iron dogs are what Natives called the first snow machines they saw. It's the world's longest and most grueling snow-mobile chal-lenge. Todd's a four-time champ at the two-thousand-mile physical, mechanical, and mental competition. One of the times he and his wife do kiss is at the starting line of the race each year.

If he wasn't out there competing for a couple of weeks or getting his equipment and himself ready for the next run, he was working up on the Slope. He was here and there. He wasn't participating in what Sarah was doing unless she needed to parade him around. He wasn't a guy who liked to be the center of attention. He's an Alaskan, through and through. At home or at a party, Todd was as exciting as a pail of water.

At his cabin? He's a different man. It was a beauti-ful setup he had out on Safari Lake. A little house with a peaked tin roof. Two bedrooms upstairs; downstairs, a mudroom, a nice little kitchen, couches, and a dish TV. I was alone with Todd at the cabin once before; and I spent time there with Bristol and her dad; and alone with Bristol a few times. Todd, Track, and I spent time there together as well. Sarah had never gone along on these occasions. She wasn't the outdoorsy type.

Todd relaxed when he was there, but even in his most mellow state Todd was difficult to read. With my male relatives, it was pretty easy. What you saw was what you got.

It was the end of August 2008. My dad, my uncle Mike, and I were out in Delta Junction for ten days, looking for sheep. After being skunked, it was time to head home. We had a six-hour ride in the trucks ahead of us.

Once I'd gotten my quad into the back of my truck, I hopped in the cab and picked up my cell. Bristol was only five months along, but we'd been out of contact for fourteen days.

I had about a dozen voice mails. Shit. My hand shook as I put the cell to my ear.

I connected with voice mail. Bristol's lungs sure were healthy. Clearly she wasn't in the hospital having a baby, or worse.

Get back right away! she screamed into the phone. They chose Sarah! She's been picked by McCain!

Holy Christ.

Then Sarah's message: Levi, I need you here. Now. We're all going to Minnesota to the convention. I'm the one.

Then Bristol. Sarah. Bristol.

Sarah told the world that her being chosen was God's plan. It would be the first time I had ever heard her mention the fella. Whether the message originated from heaven or from Arizona, the content was the same. Sarah was going to be the Republicans' nominee for vice president of the United States.

It was unreal. Maybe I should have been excited, but I wasn't. I liked my life just as it was. Slow and easy. I didn't want anything to do with a presidential campaign. I worried about Bristol. How would Sarah's expectant daughter fit in? The Palin kids had some experience with the media since their mom was a governor. I had not, and it wasn't something I was looking forward to.

8

Too Much Information

There I sat, looking out the window of a private jet, with a bird's-eye view of Alaska. We left the shining glaciers behind and I was thinking, WTF?

Heaths, Palins, and one Johnston had been transported from Wasilla and Anchorage in a four-car motorcade to the airport. The streets all around us had been blocked off. We were rolling along, the only cars on the road. Everyone was excited, bouncing around, babbling. Not me. I had gotten into one of the black cars and felt my skin start to tighten up like shrinking clothes. I was nervous and nauseous. Half way to the airport, I had to ask the driver to pull off so I could puke.

Once on the plane, I held it together although I still wasn't right. It was some sort of I'm-freaking-out illness. I was being transported in a fucking Learjet with a flight attendant to the Republican National Convention, where my girlfriend's mother would be accepting the nomination for the vice presidency of the United States.

That was not your normal situation.

We touched down in Minneapolis and drove in yet another motorcade through huge intersections blocked off in all directions by many cops. My car messed up the smooth routine when it pulled over to allow me to once again barf.

We motorcaded to the hotel with one last stop along the way so I could hurl what little was left in my stomach.

Once I was finally on solid ground, I seemed to improve. At our hotel, someone walked into our bedroom without knocking and said, We leave for the airport in fifteen minutes.

Airport?!

It turned out we weren't flying anywhere. Thank God. The Palin crowd would be welcoming the McCains as they came off their plane at some damned different airport. I had no idea what the hell was going on, where we'd been, and where we were off to. And I'm this guy who can sense true north wherever I am.

I made it all the way to our newest destination with no hurling stops.

Our handlers herded us out onto a tarmac at an airport in the Twin Cities. I looked around. Snipers were on every roof, dozens of them. It was like a *Rambo* movie. The sharpshooters were in black. It was intense. I pointed them out to Bristol, who took my arm.

The plane we were welcoming taxied over to us. The

door opened and I watched a small, old man come down the steps. He hugged Sarah and several others. My head was spinning as he strode up to me.

Hello, Levi. John McCain was talking to me.

Senator, I said.

Glad to meet you, son.

He grabbed my hand, turned it palm up. Those, he observed, are some hardworking hands.

Conversation over.

Remember, I was the kid who couldn't give a book report in the third grade. One time an announcer had interviewed me after a hockey game; that was my exposure to this world. What had I been roped into? Until Sarah was governor, I couldn't have told you the name of my state's governor. Now I might be eighteen but, like everyone I knew, I ignored politics.

This was a fucking big deal, you know?

The Alaska party—more than a dozen of us—was taken back to our own floor at the Minneapolis Downtown Hilton. The McCains had the floor above. Some woman led me and Bristol down the hall and into Sarah and Todd's suite. They had these two bedrooms with a living room in between.

Skirts, shoes, pearl necklaces were in their living room. Clotheshorse Bristol's big eyes got that liquid look that always made her look so innocent. As cute as that crazy kid Piper, who was bouncing off the walls herself.

When Bristol and I were freshman, she never ever cared

about clothes. She liked to wear hoodies. She changed when she was in tenth, eleventh grade. It became all 7s and Paige jeans—Paige, the designer, is a Wasilla girl—and North Face shells in every damned color they came in. This girl wasn't athletic—she was on the basketball C team. Her sole sport was shopping. She'd diva'd up. The first time I wanted to take her hunting, she couldn't go until she had her outfit. Boots by Juicy Couture. We were at Nordstrom in downtown Anchorage. I picked up the first boot I saw. Dafney Smith, full-grain black-leather model. $340. It looked like a damned motorcycle boot. Bristol decided on four pairs of rain boots. I was buying all this expensive shit for her to go sit in a bear stand.

In Minneapolis now the Wasilla fashionista was pawing through pants, a bracelet, belts. What do you think, Levi? Ooooh, look at this!

My pile was there as well, and so were Todd's new duds and Track's and the male cousins'. And Piper's, Willow's, Sarah's. The National Republican Committee had gone shopping for us. Did the Secret Service sniff out all our sizes? No one was insulted at the suggestion that we hayseeds couldn't even dress ourselves.

Versace socks. $80. Are you kidding me? I pulled them on. Pretty nice actually.

Standing there in my new socks, I was pulling out a pinch of chew when Sarah walked in and pulled me over to the corner:

No chew, do you hear? I don't want to see any spitters.

She took the plastic cup I was holding and threw it in the trash. I decided I'd have a heart attack with nothing in my cheek for three days. I was addicted to chew. I plowed through a McCain campaign person and a guard of some sort to make an emergency trip down to the newsstand in the lobby for $20 worth of gum. Not the same but better than nothing. I got a few boxes of mints, too.

I was chomping away on Big Red chewing gum as I walked back into the suite. Sarah got ahold of me again and for the second time pulled me over to fill me in on what was obvious. I was there for only one reason—I was Bristol's baby daddy. The McCain folks had written a statement for Sarah and Todd to announce that Bristol was pregnant. They had run it by Sarah, who'd made changes. The McCain people ignored her corrections and put out their original draft on Monday, the first night of the convention. Sarah couldn't believe they'd do such a thing—ignore her input.

We have been blessed with five wonderful children who we love with all our heart and mean everything to us. Our beautiful daughter Bristol came to us with news that as parents we knew would make her grow up faster than we had ever planned. We're proud of Bristol's decision to have her baby and even prouder to become grandparents. As Bristol faces the responsibilities of adulthood, she knows she has our unconditional love and support.

Bristol and the young man she will marry are going to realize very quickly the difficulties of raising a child, which is why they will have the love and support of our entire family. We ask the media to respect our daughter and Levi's privacy as has always been the tradition of children of candidates.

The report of Bristol's pregnancy had created quite the stir back in Wasilla, I was told. It seemed that every person named Levi was getting calls from the press all over the country, or maybe the world, wanting to know if he was *the* Levi.

This real Levi was clueless.

Then someone got to my mom, who said her son was the Levi they were looking for.

The Republicans' next decision was that everyone would cool off about the pregnancy if I was engaged to Bristol. So Sarah told everyone Bristol and I *were* engaged. If I wasn't engaged the day before, I don't think Sarah should have been the one to decide I was that day.

Maybe Bristol.

Not her mother.

Keep quiet, Sarah said to me when we bumped into each other. Say nothing.

Got it. Yes, ma'am. What was I going to say anyway? And to who? We all were under guard. But weren't the guards on our team?

In a couple of hours, I would be introduced to the public as the fiancé of Bristol Palin.

It finally was Wednesday night in the Twin Cities, the evening for Sarah to give her acceptance speech. Bristol and I and Piper had stayed in the hotel for two days, watching movies. Now, we three and the rest of the family were being gathered together by our handlers like we were cattle at a roundup.

Our appearances were checked a final time—Levi, straighten your lapel!—and we were off in yet another motorcade. We got out of the Lincoln town car at the rear of the venue, were taken through a back door, and escorted right to our seats.

Sarah was peeled off as soon as we were through that back entrance; it was Bristol, me, Piper, and the others up in a box. Meghan McCain would say in her 2010 *Dirty Sexy Politics*: I couldn't help but zero in on Levi, who was almost unrecognizable . . . the transformation was incredible. Whoa.

Stay here, we were told, until we come and get you at the end.

Like, where could we go? Where the hell were we? You're not lost unless you care where you are. A fellow woodsman Daniel Boone, had said that. I *did* care.

I sat there wide-eyed, chewing away at my gum. I didn't

know where to look, what to do. My stomach was empty or I would again have been in trouble.

I didn't usually care so much how I looked, but I'd been fussed over so much that I couldn't help but think about it. Club McCain had decided we pale-faced Alaska kids needed sprayed-on tans. They forgot about it or changed their minds. Instead, there I was—me, the recently announced baby daddy to-be, a teenager from Wasilla—made up for Christ's sake and under the gaze of a million sets of TV-viewing eyes. It felt like a meat market; I was wondering if the Chippewa would storm in any moment, searching for scalps. They wouldn't find many, not there; all the heads I saw below were bald Republican guys'.

I should have been at the rink practicing my slap shot, or on some fishy water with a rod, but, no, I was on display like a prize pig. Or Bristol was. Especially Bristol. I was this silent guy standing next to her, unable to protect her, while she hauled around her infant brother. Sarah wanted Trig in his oldest sister's arms for a reason. The blue baby blanket trailing down the front of Bristol's dress concealed the five-month baby bump. Even though the whole damn nation knew it was there.

The band was playing and there she was, Sarah, onstage, looking brilliant. Hot. Under control. Sarah was dynamite. She started to speak and I couldn't believe it was her, this woman I knew so well from back in Wasilla.

The crowd went wild.

Her speech was perfect.

The audience almost fell off their chairs with delight.

I don't know who wrote that talk, I told her that night when we were all back in the hotel and I was popping open a Diet Coke for her, but I'm impressed. Sarah was no newcomer to TV, to center stage. This was different. Smooth. Tough.

I wrote it myself, she snapped. I had to change it so much, it's like a different speech.

That was new.

A few days later Team McCain would announce that they had known all along that Bristol was with child—before they signed on Sarah. My memory is that they did not and they were shaken to their bones when they found out, but it was too late to do anything. Those McCainites looked down their long noses at Bristol once they did have the information. It wasn't right, but that's not the kind of thing her mother, Sarah, worried about. It again brought back that memory of when Bristol had called her mom at work about the rumors that she had given birth to Trig. *Who cares?*

It had all been so fast. None of us had time to think it through, work out a plan, have a discussion. I was thinking the same staffer who did the clothes shopping must have picked Sarah off the shelf. I have been more diligent tracking a moose than anyone seemed to have been in choosing the Republican vice-presidential nominee. Picking Sarah happened on the last day of hunting season for nominees, it seemed to me. Only after the McCain crew told her she was their choice did someone show up in Wasilla snooping around, asking questions.

Back home, Governor Palin hadn't even told her Alaskan constituents that her daughter had a bun in the oven—and plenty of conspiracy theories around the state still said that Bristol was Trig's mom. Now Bristol had that shine—a perfect peach ripe for the picking. Unlike her mom with Trig, Bristol was showing. No question.

She and I became media fodder.

By then, the two of us were in Wasilla. Whenever we tried to watch TV, there we were. The solution was to not turn it on. That worked.

Sarah later told me that, when a McCain handler found out about the out-of-wedlock pregnancy, he thought shotgun wedding: Are they getting married this afternoon?

What, I asked, did you tell him?

Sarah looked away. She said Bristol and I could wait, get hitched in the White House.

Holy. Shit. *That* was a big deal.

9

White House Wedding, Not

Sarah hit the campaign trail, and I don't remember any discussion at all about my moving into the house. It just seemed to happen. Todd said nothing as I hauled my stuff from my bedroom in Mom's house to Bristol's bedroom. That was weird to me; it was the first place I'd ever lived other than my childhood home. Bristol gave me a sliver of space in her closet; we bought plastic bins from Walmart for the rest of my clothes. I had my socks and underwear in her closet, along with Carhartts and T-shirts, sweaters and pajamas, under the bed in the storage containers.

She had controlled the bathroom she shared with Willow; now with three of us, things were different for Bristol. Willow seemed to like it better—but Willow always was a troublemaker.

Mom was moving, too—into a duplex for her and Sadie. My mother needed cheaper housing. She was on disability; Dad gave her cash but it wasn't enough, not like it was when they were together. I started chipping in, too.

When she lost her health insurance, she started cutting her tablets in half. The breakthrough pain was a killer. She wasn't herself anymore; it was as if someone was torturing her. I helped when I could; Sadie had been and always was there for our mom. I thought for the first time about my grandmother Anna Joyce, my father's mom, and how her marriage ended after she got so sick with MS. It was hard for a spouse to deal with an unforgiving illness and raise the kids at the same time. I wondered if that was what had happened to my own father, after he had cared for my mom all those years.

At Sarah's I was helping Bristol, too. She, now expecting, had on her shoulders the brunt of the work in that household. I cooked at the stainless-steel restaurant stove, emptied the matching dishwasher, placing the platters in the light-oak-paneled cabinets with ugly wiggly pulls that reminded me of something I couldn't stand—snakes.

The entire house had an empty feel. Wherever you went, you felt isolated in that place, with its miles of wall-to-wall carpeting everywhere but in the kitchen.

Willow cooked for herself, and Bristol made food for us and maybe some of the others, maybe not. I grilled hamburgers, chicken pieces, and reindeer-jalapeño-cheesy hot dogs. I ordered pizza from Piccolino's. Molly, Sarah's younger sister, was around, taking care of Trig when he wasn't with Sarah—and making sure someone was there for Piper. For student-teacher conferences over the years, whenever a parent was needed, it was usually Molly. Piper hung out with me and Bristol unless the little trouper was out campaigning.

Money sat on the high-shine kitchen counter, like always, so Bristol and I could buy groceries. I added my own dollars to the pot. With Sarah gone, the cash continued to appear, so it must have been Todd who doled it out.

Todd was there but he wasn't there.

He'd come in a little before midnight, never say a word to anyone or check on anything going on. He sat down in his overstuffed lounger, kicked up his feet, and turned on a basketball game with the sound off. Twenty minutes later if you walked by, you'd see he was asleep, in his recliner in the clothes he wore all day, with the silent television still on. This was where he slept every night. He got up ridiculously early. I'd go downstairs at two, three in the morning and he'd be gone. He'd got a hair up his ass and went sledding to meet up with his race partner, three and a half, four hours away.

He didn't check in with Sarah before checking out. We'd wake up and, Hey, where did Todd go?

In September I got the call from my dad's buddy on the Slope. I've got a position coming up for you, he said. This is a great job.

I was like, Right on.

111

In the meantime, I had been working the shutdown at control center in Port Valdez, the south end of the Trans Alaska Pipeline System. Valdez is a five-hour drive from Wasilla; it's Alaska's northernmost ice-free harbor.

I wasn't making huge amounts of money. Nineteen bucks an hour. I had to pay for my own keep; the Slope job would be a much better deal when it came open.

I was thankful for the Valdez job. I was a roustabout, replacing gaskets where the sections of the four-foot-diameter pipe joined together—maintenance work. I was removing nuts, slipping in a ring to seal the junction, and putting the nuts back on. It gave me time to dream about the baby—and wait for my high-paying North Slope job.

My mom and sister drove down, bringing Bristol, to visit. I'd hoped that, with Mom and Sadie driving, it wouldn't be so bad for my babe. Along the way, though, she'd text and call, unhappy with the distance. She wasn't feeling so hot. My mom told me years later that it felt as if Bristol was scared to let her guard down, allow herself to have fun and relax, trust us. We were going to be family after all. Mom could never understand that. She tried to get close to her and hoped we would all have a warm relationship. We're a hugging family and I know they aren't.

What was odd—maybe not so strange—was that Bristol told me she loved my mom. Bristol had that kind of personality I'd seen in kids who were adopted and had trouble with relationships.

———

I was having my own bonding problems. In October of that year, 2008, ASRC started laying off employees in both Valdez and on the Slope. I was one who got a pink slip. ASRC did offer me two other jobs. I could work in Cook Inlet, close to my babe, or I could go into the electrical apprenticeship program at Milne Point, on the Slope. That Milne Point job was perfect for me; it led to a career; the pay was excellent, even as an apprentice. With Bristol expecting in two months though, I was uncomfortable being far away. Valdez was bad enough.

That night Sarah, campaigning with Elisabeth Hasselbeck from *The View* in Florida, called about the clothes we'd worn at the convention. We were to not wear them anymore; people were complaining that they cost too much. I could see that Sarah was in a flap, going on about this, when Bristol got a word in, telling her mom about my two job offers. Sarah broke in, Tell him I said to take the apprentice job. It's perfect. He'll be sorry if he lets it slip through his fingers.

And she hung up.

I said to Bristol, I heard her.

Bristol still held the dead phone as she turned to me and said, It's what my dad always did. I'll be okay.

Her hangdog expression said different.

I went to Kenai the first week in November, filled out W-4s, then flew to the Slope.

They knew who I was, knew my dad. Everyone in the state was aware that I was the governor's daughter's baby daddy-to-be.

Not that Sarah did anything to get me the job.

I'd fly up to the Slope for three, four weeks at a time. They'd bring me home to be with Bristol for a few days, then I was back to work. Normally the strict schedule was like two weeks on and two weeks off, three and three. They knew she was pregnant and I was a hard worker. They were good to me.

I was earning $1,900 a week. I worked as much as I could, pulling in the cash, as I built a nest egg for Bristol and the baby. She was talking marriage and how wonderful our lives would be. Her dreams were my dreams. I was stockpiling cash. I knew she wanted a house of her own.

Everything was going well. The journeymen, the real electricians, were fighting over me.

We were servicing outdoor lighting. The drilling pads had big pole lights. We followed a schedule to change the giant bulbs that kept this around-the-clock operation running. We were getting paid for sixteen-hour days, and they allotted five days to replace ten lights. Those lamps weigh two hundred pounds, and it took two of us to pick one up. We'd go up in a lift to reinstall the fixtures.

It was a cushy job for a semiskilled laborer. We ate great food. I didn't pay for my plane tickets up there and I didn't pay for my room. I had health insurance, a pension. I was eighteen, making great money.

Despite the perks, I couldn't wait to get back to Bristol, check out the size of our baby bump. I loved to sleep with my hand on her tummy, waiting for the kicks. I imagined a hockey game was going on in there.

There was another game going on—hide and seek. We no longer had the seclusion we'd loved in the past when, with Todd outside and Sarah either at work or holed up in her first-floor bedroom for hours, we pretty much had had the house to ourselves. Now we had the Secret Service.

They had followed us back from the convention and had been a presence ever since. Between them and Republican handlers here and there, Bristol and I and the whole family had lost all of our privacy.

The Feds didn't knock on the door when they first showed up, to let us know they were on the job and all over the property. They just took their positions, spreading out like carpenter ants.

The agents were supposed to be invisible. After a while, no one else noticed them but me. I saw them as easy as I spotted a goat or a sheep at three hundred yards. They were staked out all over the property, on the lake in back, and in the woods in front. It was like crawling spiders everywhere. I hate bugs as much as I hate snakes.

The Secret Service placed a little guardhouse at the far end of the Palins' gravel driveway. They checked out anyone they didn't recognize who pulled up in a car.

That bothered Bristol.

Inside the house it was bad for us folks used to coming and going as we chose, when we chose. Sarah's people answered the door and the phone. Questions? Ask the McCain campaign staff. Agents went with Bristol and me wherever we went, keeping an eye, talking into their little earpieces. I knew Wasilla, the back roads and shortcuts, but no matter how hard I tried, I could never shake them.

We went to Mom's and they stayed as long as we did, and so did the McCain operatives. They all came in and out of the house and seemed to melt into the corners. Sadie had loads of Palin and Johnston photos on her laptop. One day they all were gone. Did someone scrub her hard drive? It wouldn't have surprised me.

A few months before, we were just a couple of small-town Alaskan kids. Not anymore. My family had always criticized me when they thought it would help. They were the ones I trusted and listened to. I didn't need a bunch of national referees using instant replay on the evening news to analyze every little mistake I made. It was a hell of a sporting event, but it was also our lives.

I liked being unknown, Bristol pouted.

She wouldn't be in a picture unless she was sure she looked perfect. She was wearing hoodies again nine-tenths of the time, even to bed. Or a big T-shirt, and shorts. She tended to change in the bathroom. She was trying to hide from the world.

She told me, I don't like people in my business. I felt the same damn way. We both wanted our old lives back.

Sarah was the headliner. We watched her on the stump, with Trig, her accessory. It made my stomach turn to see him displayed like a designer bag, then passed off to the nanny. I also was sick in my gut when I heard the media report that people were saying—again—Trig wasn't Sarah's baby. Then I heard Sarah doing the same thing to Obama, insisting he wasn't born in Hawaii. The next time I heard her ranting on the Trig truthers, I pointed out that she was doing the same shit that made her so angry. I've seen Sarah livid, but that was the first time she looked at me that way. I said to her again, I didn't see the difference between the Obama birthers, who delighted Sarah, who she egged on— and the Trig truthers she detested.

I think, I added, that both groups are out of their minds.

I watched as Sarah's face changed from its usual tan tone to a serious pink. She opened her mouth to chew me out, thought about it, and clamped her teeth. Sarah liked to talk about anger management and controlling emotions. She worked at it herself, but you could always tell when she was serious. She colored up. No one ever noticed it under the makeup: she would get red when she got hot under the collar, on TV. Bristol didn't see it but I did.

Bristol did spot her mom's red heels. They were slick, I agreed. I could have lived for six months on what they must have set her back.

Sarah was looking good and I was on her team, but I could see she was in over her head. People were scratching their heads over her run-on sentences—whenever she spoke off-the-cuff. That was what happened when she began a sentence and lied halfway through. She hadn't figured out before she started to speak how her thought was going to end—until after she said it. All politicians lied, but she seemed not to have it down pat. She did know how to use fibbing to change the story, to turn her, the aggressor, into the victim. She was the one to feel sorry for, then—smack! She took her shot. . . .

She was stupid-smart. It fooled a lot of people.

She'd never admit she didn't know what she was talking about, or that she didn't have an answer to an easy question. It was the same deal when she tried to talk to me about hockey, acting like she knew something about strategy. She was the same way on the rare occasions when she came into the kitchen and tried to cook. The disaster was the pot's fault, the recipe was wrong, or the kids messed it up.

Bristol and I watched her on the tube and listened as she dropped her words of wisdom. It was, to me, like eating food with no taste. Lots of hissing and splattering, but the end product never seemed to have much substance. If her train of thought started going off the tracks, we could tell she was in trouble by her sudden, squeally pitch, like nails on a blackboard.

Bristol's voice was peaceful. I loved that about her.

———

One thing else I loved about her, her independence, seemed to be changing. Overnight she was needy. I noticed it when I told her I wanted to go to her checkup with her. She leaned on me, so grateful. It was like, if I hadn't told her that, she wouldn't have made it herself.

By the time of the appointment, I was worried. Everything was good physically, we were told, as Bristol entered her third trimester. I was glad to know that, but didn't understand why her mood was darkening, why she didn't seem able to cope with life. Her life.

I spent my nights giving her massages. I did whatever I could think of to make her feel good. It didn't seem to help.

She was a teenager and giving birth would end that phase of her life. It had to be scary for her, with no idea what to expect. She had just gotten to know her adult body in the past year or so, and now this.

It struck me that she might be afraid. The next time Sarah was around, maybe she could shore up her young daughter a bit, reassure her. It's not the kind of thing Sarah did, but I could ask.

In the meantime I told Bristol it was understandable that she'd be nervous—maybe that's what the aches and pains were about. Nothing physical. She cried. Palins don't cry. I'd never seen Sarah cry. Ever. Todd—never, never, never. If I did ever see him, he'd have to kill me.

This was new. Bristol asked me if I'd go get her a slushie. She had never liked those disgusting things before. And some fries, she added. From McDonald's.

If you marry me now, she said as I dried the tears from her cheeks with a Kleenex, I'll be happy.

What about the wedding in the White House? I pointed out.

Oh, yeah. Her brow crinkled. Rub my feet. In the arches.

I had a lifetime of experience with a woman in pain— my mother, who would clench her fists, curl her toes, groan while rubbing her stomach in agony. Mom bit her lip and carried on.

That is not what my Bristol was doing.

She wanted a wine cooler. No alcohol, I told her, and stopped drinking myself for the remainder of her pregnancy. I never really did drink after that.

She was annoyed when I had to go back up on the Slope, to my job at Milne Point.

I want you here. Stay and we can elope.

Babe, remember how we want to save and first buy a house?

Mmmmm. I want a place with four bedrooms. Don't leave tomorrow. Let's look at properties.

You gotta pick and choose, Bristol, one or the other. Marry today? Go to work and save for a house? Actually she didn't have to be logical, sensible. She was like a little girl, fretting about what she might be in for.

I guess I was, too.

We both needed help, but I didn't go to her family to talk about it. I couldn't turn to Willow; she was going through a wild-teenager phase and wouldn't have given a damn. Drinking, partying, smoking weed. It's what we all did growing up, but she was all attitude. You could see it in the *Sarah Palin's Alaska* episodes. God knows what they edited out. That voice of Willow's dripping with sarcasm. Swearing like Todd. She is the best looking of the Palin women. She will turn out to be the family beauty—but that mouth of hers is something.

Too bad I couldn't have asked Piper for her opinion. She was rock steady, like Denali. She was too young. So that left Sarah and Todd.

Sarah was a detached mother, hiding out in her room, and Todd was never one for discussions. I could have gone to my mom, with Bristol. It might have helped to talk it all out, but I was eighteen and teenage boys don't think that way. Bristol continued to cling to me. It was no longer a relationship of equals.

Well, you all know how it turned out. The Sarah-McCain ticket didn't quite make it to the White House. There would be no Johnston-Palin wedding in the Rose Garden.

On the day of the maverick meltdown, I went out and bought Bristol a truck as a surprise.

Two weeks before that, I had been thinking that I

needed a four-door truck for the baby, with a backseat. I got my first truck when I was sixteen—a big 350, four-door, long-bed diesel that Dad and I used together to mess around. I drove my 2002 Chevy, extended-cab short bed every day.

Bristol and I were driving by the dealer and she pointed. That's the one I want.

It's red, I said. Are you sure?

She was sure. I went back to work on the Slope during the final week of campaigning, and on Election Day I flew back to Wasilla to vote for Sarah and John. Now eighteen, this was my first time voting. Bristol had never gotten around to registering, so she never cast a ballot for her mom.

I saw that the truck was still in the dealer's window. I went in to buy it, trading in the 2002 Chevy and throwing in my summer earnings for the truck Bristol wanted. If Sarah won, I thought, the present will be a victory truck. If that doesn't happen, maybe the red would cheer up Bristol.

I loved giving her gifts. Lots of hugs and kisses.

No one inside Kendall Ford wanted to see Obama become president, except maybe me, almost. I saw that he was presidential material and I knew Sarah wasn't. Still, it would be a trip to be connected to the vice president.

All of us in the dealership were standing behind Sarah. The results started coming in—we're four hours behind the East Coast—and the manager locked the doors. It was just me and the Ford guys in there, sitting around, watching the screen, and shaking our heads. They were fucking furious. It was bad. I got on the phone with Bristol in Arizona, and then Sarah, and we were all talking.

The Ford guys eavesdropped.

It was a drubbing.

Sarah never delivered the concession speech she planned to make that night. The McCains didn't let her. That was for the best. Bristol told me her mom had written that one herself.

I left the new red truck in the Palin driveway before flying off to work for five days. Bristol found the truck there when she came home the next morning. She called to say she loved it and was even happier to finally be getting her life back.

It was all good. Well, maybe not for Sarah.

We all had to return the fancy duds the RNC bought us. I kept the Versace socks.

Bristol and I decided we'd get married in the backyard. It had been something we'd talked about up in her room before all the craziness. Bristol said she'd like me to wear my camo vest, and she'd arrive in her dad's plane.

Right. The hell with the Rose Garden, I said to her, lightening up the mood. She looked at me with those big eyes. I felt like I was drowning in a pool of water.

I want roses though, she said. Lots.

We were still in love and would raise our baby in Wasilla. Things were improving. Going back to before the stress of the campaign. Bristol seemed to be coming out of her funk, and once the baby had been born, we'd really begin our lives together.

I started planning one more hunting trip before the due date. I was making good money and could afford to take a little time off.

It was all good.

10

Tripp Easton
Mitchell Johnston

The country's going to be sorry, said Sarah
with her arms crossed and her chin on her chest, pacing
from one end of the living room to the other. A minute
later she raised her head and had that glazed Joan of Arc
look. All she needed was a mic in her hand and she'd be
belting out the national anthem. Everything was the fault
of someone else, including her kids and her husband—
Todd, who could care less if he was the one to blame for all
her woes. It was impossible for them to know what to say
that wouldn't light her short fuse.

She didn't seem to have a problem with me but, for
everyone else in the house, it was hell. They all had to
walk on eggshells. She'd pout and act wounded, then she
attacked. She even went after Piper. That was inexcusable.

I'd still never seen Sarah cry, not even now, when she'd
lost. She was furious, not sad. Sadness might mean she had
something to do with what had happened.

She said Obama cheated to win. She talked as if they

were the only two running. Not Biden, not McCain. Sarah and Barack, in hand-to-hand combat.

Whatever you may think of Obama, he seemed to be an inquisitive guy. I'd never felt that Sarah was all that curious about the world outside Alaska, and I sure never saw her read a book. Not that I did much of that either. But I wasn't gunning for the White House.

On the morning of the day of Sarah's acceptance speech at the Republican National Convention, as she had raced out the door of our suite after checking on Track, I had asked her, "What does a vice president do exactly?

Take over—she had smiled—when the president dies.

Sarah was still governor of Alaska, but after the taste of national celebrity, it was just too much of a small-town job for her.

There's that line my grandpa Joel used to say: You can't go back to the farm after you've seen gay Paree. I didn't understand what the heck he was talking about for years, that sometimes there's no going back. There was just no way that Sarah would lock herself back up here. The genie was out of the bottle. And now there was money to be made.

The wealth and the self-importance affected Sarah and Todd, not in a good way. It was like their shit didn't stink. The kids had traveled, been exposed to people and places that they would never have seen otherwise. They changed, too.

The whole experience opened my eyes as well. I'd be happy if I never left my home state again.

It was the middle of November 2008. I was pulling ninety-, hundred-hour weeks working on the oil patch. I was piling up the cash. No hunting, no fishing, no snow machining, no hockey.

Sarah's anger at the injustice of the election started to wear on Bristol. The bad vibes were contagious. I could only be there for a couple of days and nights at a stretch, but it was enough time to get plenty yelled at. Not by Sarah, never Sarah. It was Bristol who shouted, You're a horrible person, Levi—then whispered, Let's get married this weekend.

Dad and I were walking through Sportsman's Warehouse while I was chatting with Bristol on my phone. A couple of kids passed, recognized me, and started making comments loud enough for Bristol to pick up.

Levi, I hear you! Screwing around with those fucking girls. What the hell is going on? Damn it. You fucking bastard. . . .

I couldn't quiet her. Dad heard her. His jaw dropped.

This was on a day when we were getting along.

Things went from bad to worse. Bristol started saying

that her mom wanted her to dump me. To my face, Sarah acted all nice.

Are you sure, I asked Bristol, your mom said that to you?

No, my mom didn't; my dad told me Sarah wants you gone.

Todd. Now when his wife and I talked, he would watch me like a bear with raised guard hairs. I started wondering if I was imagining things. I decided to keep away from Sarah, at least when Todd was around—and then I just tried to keep out of everyone's way, to be safe.

It didn't help.

Todd told Bristol that if she left me, he would buy her a brand-new car. Bristol thought Sarah was making him say that. Then Bristol would say that getting married would end all the problems. My head started to feel like it would explode whenever I was at the house. I couldn't make any sense of it.

Sarah was often on the phone in her room, talking to her agent about her book contract, about TV possibilities. I want to be rich, she'd say to herself out loud on a trip to and from the kitchen, make millions. She was sure she could give $100,000 speeches. What was she doing back here in Alaska, she would ask herself, staying in the same place when she could be moving forward?

Bristol wore the same mood. I don't like living here

anymore, she told me one morning as I was massaging her shoulders. You aren't doing enough for me.

I cooked. I loaded and unloaded the dishwasher. Garbage out. Errands. I did the laundry. I held little Trig in my arms, diapered him. So what was the bitch?

Back on the Slope, I would think as I fell asleep, I do not want to live my life like this.

I imagined a Bristol-free life.

My mother, of all people, did not help my situation. In a new and unsuccessful attempt to manage her pain, she'd been given an implanted morphine pump that was meant to replace her pills. The pump helped but there was still breakthrough pain.

With the divorce, and her insurance no longer covering the Oxy, Mom, unable to work, was strapped for cash. It was then that one of the kids who used to play hockey in our backyard got himself—and then Mom—into trouble.

He'd hung around our house years before—long enough to know Mom took these meds. She had suspected that he'd stolen some, and she kept them in a safer place after that.

While Mom was wondering what she was going to do when her meds ran out, he called to see if she had any extra. Mom sent him packing, but he persisted while Mom's debts continued to rise.

The guy kept at her, asking for her Oxy. Mom didn't know that this guy was an addict, had been busted by the cops, and, in exchange for a reduced sentence, had become a snitch. He called, although she had never given him her cell number. He stopped by, asking. Finally, Mom relented—the biggest and stupidest mistake of her life. She agreed to sell ten pills and met him in the Target parking lot to do the deal. She knew it was illegal; she was desperate. Her plan was to use the extra cash to purchase the less expensive Oxy prescribed for her through her pain clinic that she'd had no money to buy. She was selling the pills for twice what she had to pay for them at the pharmacy.

The guy kept calling; twice more Mom sold him ten tablets and was able to take the cash and pick up her prescription refill.

Mom was set up. The cops recorded every part of the deal. Law enforcement came in mid-December, arrested her, and ripped the house apart. They found her Walgreens vial of Oxy that she kept in her purse. That was it.

She had been taken away in cuffs. Sadie was bawling into the phone. That was the first either of us knew what was going on. Mom pleaded guilty at her arraignment, and they let her return home and await sentencing months later.

She had seen the ads a criminal-law attorney, Rex Butler, ran, and she wrote a four-page letter asking for his assistance even though she had no money to pay him. Rex had the heart to take her case *pro bono* and represented her at her sentencing. She could have gotten twenty-five years in prison for her six felony counts, but the charges were reduced to one felony trafficking count, for selling thirty pills of a medication that was prescribed to her, that she'd bought at Walgreens. Mom got three years in prison and three years' probation. She spent four months in the medical wing at the state's women's prison and was released due to medical necessity. She wore an ankle monitor and was confined to our house for three years less time served. She could leave the house once each week for short, specified periods like shopping and doctors' appointments, as well as drug testing—although of course she was on Oxy and had a pump. I never understood how they worked all that out.

Because she was on prescription meds, the probation department would not allow her to use her car. She had been driving for a couple of decades while taking these pills, but they worried about liability. My bighearted sister Sadie who had just graduated high school got in the habit of caring for Mom. Sadie should have been thinking about her own future. She was a firecracker and it was hard to get her to listen to her big brother on what was best for her.

What a disaster.

A couple of months later, Todd's half sister Diana Palin got herself in trouble with the law as well. She brought her four-year daughter along when she broke into the same house twice. She was charged with misdemeanor theft and criminal trespass.

Neither Todd nor Sarah showed up for her trial. The victim of the break-in broke down in tears as he asked the judge to go light on her. What a generous guy, really.

Diana was serving time at the same time Sarah told the media we Johnstons were trailer trash. While I was living in her house. Bristol said nothing. I kept my mouth shut. I'm not proud of that.

My mom's arrest put a huge crack in my already choppy relations with the Palins. Bristol and I were constantly fighting. Though we would always make up and talk about getting married. The only person in the Palin family I could get along with was Piper. I could imagine being a dad to a sweet little thing like her, except I would guess Bristol and Willow might have been like her at some point. What happened?

Bristol wasn't there, in mind or spirit. She and her huge tum-tum were napping upstairs in our bedroom. Sarah was behind closed doors in her own private space. I had no idea where Todd was. And Willow? Probably hiring herself out as a PI.

One day I was there for the kids while Trig's nanny went shopping. I'd just changed his diaper and fed him his bottle. He was dozing on my arm as Piper, sitting next to us, was working her way through a book. She and I were close, and as she sounded out the words with some help from me, she was leaning against me. I looked down at the top of her head, her hair, and thought what fun it would be to be a dad to a child like her, a girl. Maybe after our little son was born. Maybe once we were set in a house. If everything worked out.

It was like Piper was reading my mind. She stopped her reading, closed her book.

Levi? She looked up at me.

Yes, Little Piper?

No matter what happens, no matter how old or young I am, no matter where my mom is, or my dad, or my brothers and sisters, I'm always going to be your baby's special aunt.

Well said, little child.

I suggested that Piper go upstairs, brush her teeth, and get ready for bed. When she got to the landing, she turned around and gave me that big wave she learned to do during the campaign.

Christ.

It was Christmas Day 2008. Bristol was huge; a photo of that belly would cut off at the knees the Trig truthers who insisted she was his mom.

This was the one day of the year that the Palins went to church. Bristol didn't want to go and I stayed home with her.

We'd already exchanged gifts. The month before, she had handed me a list of the shit she wanted to have on hand as soon as she wasn't pregnant. The usual Paige jeans and some 7s. I surprised her with a chocolate fountain. She loved chocolate and had been putting on too much weight so she had to stop eating candy. I knew she'd look forward to using the thing in three weeks, as soon as the baby was born. She went crazy over it, my God. More North Face shells, the newest colors. $110 a pop. A Coach purse and two pairs of shoes to make up for the tanning bed I wasn't getting her.

She had always looked sexy in colorful camo undies and bras and bikini panties in animal prints. I appreciated them myself, being a hunter. I was sure to buy her some in the unpregnant-Bristol size. I'd asked Willow the sizes. She had no trouble delivering the intel.

I gave Todd a Ski-Doo shirt and hat. I meant it to be a joke since Todd hated Ski-Doo and had an Iron Dog sponsorship from Arctic Cat. I gave Piper a kid makeup kit along with a pink Ski-Doo chick hat that she adored. She wore it everywhere.

Todd was irritated by Piper's hat, which served him right since he gave me nothing.

So I was surprised when we got back from visiting my dad and Lisa, then Mom and Sadie, that Todd called to me as Bristol and I were going up to bed. He asked if I wanted to go snow machining the next morning with him and Piper and Willow. They planned to overnight at the cabin in Petersville.

It sounded good; Todd only seemed to have a beef with me when Sarah was around. And Willow was okay when she was with her dad.

I was worried though about leaving Bristol.

I told her I wasn't going to go, but she insisted, wanted me to get some time with Todd. I don't know whether Bristol was trying to get rid of me or really hoped Todd and I would become closer. I didn't care at that point. I was just happy for a break.

I also was getting a reprieve from the wedding series she loved to watch with me. It had been getting worse, this fascination with marriage. I saw so many of these shows that I could be a wedding planner, doing anything from divas to redneck weddings—with the bride and groom wrestling pigs in a mud pit.

Before I left that morning, I made Bristol lunch and left a surprise box of her favorite candy, Almond Roca, under her pillow. I loaded my machine in my truck. Bristol wasn't due for another three weeks. At least that was the plan.

I got the call at the cabin at 10:00 p.m. Todd and I jumped out of our chairs like a couple of prairie dogs and sledded back to my truck. Before he turned around to go back to Willow and Piper, Todd put his left hand on my shoulder and shook my right hand. If the circumstances had been different, I think he and I would have been friends.

He went back to the cabin and stayed there with the girls until the following day.

I gunned it all the way back to Wasilla, praying I would get there in time. I had over an hour's drive ahead of me. I realized I was so hyper that I hadn't gotten much info from

Bristol. I didn't know how far she was into labor. I just figured if I drove ninety I might make it there in time. Well, sixty.

I kept that pace as I saw ahead of me the lights of Wasilla. I closed in on the Mat-Su Regional Medical Center. It looked like the stacked cubes of a Pueblo community plopped on the Alaskan snow and topped here and there with pyramids.

Right now it looked like heaven.

Once I got inside the lobby, I headed straight for the Birthing Center. I had taken this same route eight months before, for Trig's birth.

This was different.

This was Bristol's and my baby.

Sarah's head swiveled when I walked into Bristol's suite. I walked over to the other side of the bed.

Sarah looked like the weight of the world had been lifted off her shoulders.

Levi's here, she said, leaning over Bristol and patting her hair. Isn't that great?

Bristol shook her mother's hand off her head.

I didn't know it then, but it would be another five hours before my son was born.

Sarah, Bristol, and I were the only ones there. No one had called my *trailer-trash* father, mother, and sister. Why didn't I? I guess I didn't want to ruffle any feathers.

Levi, Sarah broke into my thoughts. *Thank you* for getting here so fast, she said, leaning over Bristol to touch my arm. I was John Wayne who had just ridden in to rescue the pretty lady in distress. Sarah could have been the one in labor. She looked a mess, hair stuck to her forehead, glasses askew. A little like the librarian who just let down her hair.

Poor Bristol was twisting and turning, throwing her body side to side. She grabbed for me, hit my chin. I kissed her forehead. She smiled up at me, and then she screamed.

Oh my God. My babe was in serious pain.

It was her first delivery and she was only a girl. She screamed again. I mean flat-out screamed.

Where was the epidural? I called the nurse. Bring that epidural in here right now. Bristol was wailing, cussing up a storm, bitching at her mother.

We need that damn epidural! Now I'm yelling, too. Sarah and I were trying to talk Bristol down and it made her angry. Again, she went after her mom, verbally and then physically. Sarah ducked.

Calm down, babe. Calm down. Breathe. Breathe. Bristol lay back and squeezed my hand until it was bloodless.

The doc came in and gave her the epidural. Then she was all sweet and nice and messed up out of her mind.

Then she passed out, asleep.

Sarah and I looked at each other, took a deep breath together, and smiled. We'd broken the filly with good teamwork.

I was starving. Sarah suggested I run over to the Taco Bell. It was her favorite fast food. I knew she loved their quesadillas and asked if she wanted me to bring one back for her.

I don't think I could manage it, she said.

When I got back fifteen minutes later, Bristol was still sleeping.

She woke up an hour later with me at her side. She was sweaty, exhausted—and so beautiful.

It would be three more hours before the doc said those wonderful words to me: She's good to go.

Bristol wanted to push. Together we were panting that baby out. How the hell does anyone manage to do this all by themselves? Tripp took his time, finally arrived after six hours of labor. The cord had been wrapped around his short, little neck twice.

One look at this baby boy—a miracle!—and I knew my life would never be the same.

I was given scissors to cut the clamped cord. What I needed was an oxygen mask. My fingers were jelly. I was overwhelmed, grabbed on to the rail of Bristol's bed with one hand, and passed Sarah the scissors.

Snip. Baby Tripp was on his own.

I would have loved a little Piper of my own, but when we found out we were going to have a boy, we already had the name picked out—actually way before Bristol had even conceived. Trip was a character in one of those psycho scrambler motocross films. Trip Carlyle. It had a nice ring to it. Bristol added the second "p." Easton Mitchell? Easton was my favorite hockey-stick supplier. It was the name I liked—Easton—and so did Bristol. We decided on Mitchell because it's Todd's middle name. I thought he'd like that. It also was John Wayne's real middle name, Marion Mitchell Morrison. I never mentioned that, about Duke, to Bristol, I must admit.

The nurse put my cleaned-up son in Bristol's arms and my world was complete. The new mom relaxed for the first time in hours . . . months. All our worries about how we'd do disappeared in an instant. I felt as if it was the most natural thing in the world. We were a trio, a team, ready to face all challenges. For the first time since my cousin Matt Craver had died when I was fourteen and he was sixteen—his car had slipped on ice and he was T-boned in an intersection—I found myself crying, cradling my son. Oh, Matt, how I miss you. How can I ever put this child down? I wanted to spend every minute of my life like that. I felt a new attachment, as strong as I'd had with my cousin, yet different, something I'd never before known.

I vowed to protect this little thing forever. It was a new kind of love for me. Nothing could ever destroy it. With his birth, it was the same world but it seemed like a fresh start.

Todd and Piper and Willow showed up a few hours later, and then Sammy Becker and my mom and Sadie—and Bristol's other pals. The new mom was discharged that night, and the next day my dad came over to the Palins to see his first grandchild.

Everything was good.

In 2009, almost a year after Tripp's arrival, the AP and just about every other news source in America reported that Sarah said it was shameful that I was absent when her daughter Bristol Palin gave birth to Tripp. What about lying when your kid knows it's a lie? It's like a lesson that that's an okay thing to do. How could you ever respect a person who does that? I know politicians misspeak, but I figured they'd tell the truth when they were back with family—talking about the birth of their grandson, for God's sake.

I could not believe it when Bristol chimed in, intimating that I wasn't there. At least she was a little wishy-washy about it. Caught in the middle. Or maybe that epidural was far stronger than I realized.

The shame is on *you*, Sarah. Then you say you helped the doctor deliver Tripp. The cutting of the cord?

I will admit I was unable to do it myself.

11

Mommy Sarah

Now three of us were living in Bristol's upstairs bedroom. Before the baby was born, Bristol and I had painted her walls a pale taupe-y color. It had been blue and some other color before that. She liked to redo the room, loved a new color. The first day home in that nice fresh room was smooth sailing because Bristol had put in mega-hours of child care with her younger siblings.

We were in the living room when Sarah came down the stairs. I was burping Trig. Bristol was rocking the newest Johnston in her arms. She saw her mom and said to Tripp, but really for her mom, Here's comes Grandma. Do you want to say hi to Grandma?

Sarah wasn't interested in this exchange, at least not the way it was unfolding.

I do not, she announced, want to be called Grandma. Tripp can call me Mommy Sarah.

She turned on her heel and walked into her bedroom and closed the door.

Bristol, who had been holding her breath, now let it

out. She whooped and said, That's too funny. Sarah can't stand the thought of being a grandmother.

I didn't join in. I was beginning to feel uncomfortable.

My mother, sister, and father had not been told that Bristol was in labor, and afterward, Bristol said that Sarah didn't want them in the Palin house. Mom had told me since I was a little kid dealing with a bully in the neighborhood, Treat tough guys with kindness. I remember the boy who was terrorizing all the kids, even the girls. My mom invited him for dinner and a sleepover! I just about died, tried to go over to my cousin's. It changed that guy's life. He's now one of my best friends.

I was giving Bristol the alone time she needed. Lots of naps. I was seeing around the edges the old Bristol, the one I loved. She was going to breast-feed. It was good for Tripp and I had urged her to take the Breast-Feeding Success! course at the hospital. I'd go, too, I told her, when I wasn't working. It didn't happen. Sarah hadn't breast-fed Trig, but I'd been telling my babe all along, It's a great idea; let's plan to do that. I was thinking she'd enjoy it.

She did her best and it was all good for a while. Tripp was a natural.

Not so fast. Bristol said it hurt too much so she pumped and we gave Tripp bottles.

Sometimes Bristol was a big baby herself.

———

My kindness-to-bullies campaign was a failure. Sarah, when she showed up, was mean to everyone. Maybe now me in particular. She'd done a total turnaround since the baby came home. Bristol told me, as she popped another Almond Roca into her mouth, that her father told her that he and her mom wanted me to sleep on the couch downstairs, not in her room.

Okay.

Bristol was crabby before the baby's birth; I didn't know what to call her after. I found myself shielding Tripp from it all, locating corners where he and I could be alone.

When the baby woke up during the night, I changed him and he and I tiptoed downstairs where Todd was dead to the world in his recliner. When Tripp finished his bottle, he got his own forty winks in my arms. We three males overnighted in the living room.

Bristol didn't like that Tripp slept downstairs with Todd and me. She also didn't want him in her room when she was resting. She didn't like me to fuss over him when she said he should be sleeping.

You're feeding him the wrong way, she pointed out, and at the wrong time.

He doesn't need so much burping.

He's fussing; do something.

Don't keep picking him up.

What the—?

Mommy Sarah, back in her old role as governor, was home midafternoon as usual. One day, she had walked in through the garage door, into the kitchen and across the stretched-out living room. Bristol was in Todd's lounger, bouncing Trig on her knee. I had my son on the couch, on my chest. Sarah came over, kissed little Trig, who was eight months older.

Bristol held him up to give him to her.

Nah, Sarah said, kidding around. I don't want the retarded one.

I gave her a look. A buddy of mine has a brother with Down's. I was familiar with the syndrome. Crosby coached his brother's hockey team and I was assistant coach at the Alaska Special Olympics. I loved doing it for these affectionate, appreciative kids. I loved doing it for myself. These children make the rest of us wonder what is our problem. Down's is no joke, especially for families who don't have the means to hire special-needs experts.

Sarah winked at me like old times, came over, and took Tripp from my arms. Then she coaxed out a smile. From both of us. Back then, Sarah could make me smile even if I didn't feel like it.

I went back to work on the Slope, leaving Tripp behind with his mama. I knew she'd take good care of him. I thought she might be right that I spoiled him.

I wasn't gone long enough to find out.

All hell broke loose on January 5—Tripp was nine days old—when the Alaska media found out I wasn't a high school graduate. They figured Sarah had got me the cushy job. I knew I should have had a diploma or GED to be in the apprentice electrician program. I called Dad, who said, Go see so-and-so and resign right now. End the controversy. It'll hurt Sarah if you don't.

I did what he told me before it got any worse for Sarah. I quit that day. I was like, I'm done. Later.

I was off the Slope and back home three days later, looking forward to caring for my little one.

At the airport, I got into my truck and headed over to the Palins'. I'd be with Tripp in a few minutes.

Bristol greeted me at the door.

I think, she told me, we should take a break.

You know what, Bristol, you're right. But what about my boy?

I was the same guy I'd been a year before, six months before. What had happened?

She stood over me, explaining how it was my fault as I spent a half day packing up my crap and carrying it to my truck. You've been unfair, she said. She accused me of being out to get her, trying to make it look like she was not a good mother. She was the victim. And, as usual, I was seeing other girls behind her back.

I saw only a glimpse of Sarah as she went into her room and shut the door.

A couple of weeks later *People* magazine reported we'd split up. They quoted me saying it was mutual. I guess it was except that I was the one with the most to lose.

I found myself out of work, out of a place to live. I had this little one I was crazy about, and I needed to figure out how to support him. Eighteen years didn't seem to provide enough life experience to draw on to handle the situation I was in.

If Ice was still alive, I'd have gone over and taken the rottweiler for a run in the woods.

I had walked away from my junior year in high school. No college; no hockey.

I had let my dad and myself down.

I was screwed.

The one positive thing to come out of the whole deal was that I got my friends back. Bristol had not wanted me to see them, and at the time I'd gone along with that. Now they were there for me, as comforting as always. My uncle Robbie tried to set me up in a little cabin in the woods. It didn't work out so I moved back in with Mom and Sadie. I dropped off diapers and formula and shit to Bristol. I had money saved up from six months of eighty-hour weeks and began to think about renting my own place, maybe with Dom.

About a month later, I got a midnight call from Bristol. She was alone with Tripp at her parents' house on the lake.

LEFT: My parents met at my grandma's hair salon, E-Z Clippers in Wasilla, in 1986. Mom cut Dad's hair. He was chicken to ask her out and got his sister, Rene, to do it for him. Here they are, half a year later.

BELOW: Littlest Levi. Me at six weeks with my grandma Myrna.

A fat little me at thirteen months trying out trout fishing with my dad. We were at King Lake near home, just after spring breakup.

Practicing for my future no-frontal-nudity *Playgirl* gig.

That is me, #175, and Dad. Kitty Cat racing. You know, little-guy snowmobile racing.

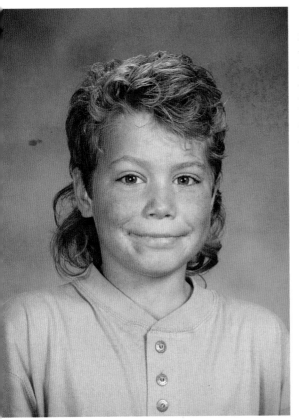

LEFT: Here's the mullet I wore from second grade till I was eighteen— when I gave it up for the Republican cause; Sarah insisted I cut it for the 2008 convention.

BELOW: I'm in the middle here with Matt Craver and Tyson Sampson. We were using .410 shotguns to hunt grouse. Matt died in a car crash at sixteen. We all miss him a lot.

ABOVE: Mike Craver took this shot of Dad and me in Paxson, Alaska. It was my first caribou. It made for great stews, burgers, and steaks.

BELOW: Ice the dog and me on Grandpa Tim's airboat. This is on the Big Susitna River and before the mishap with Ice and Uncle Robbie Sampson on the Little Willow.

RIGHT: This is at Anchorage's old Tesoro Sports Center. I was team captain and I am receiving the MVP award in the Pee Wee League. I had scored twice to win the state championship.

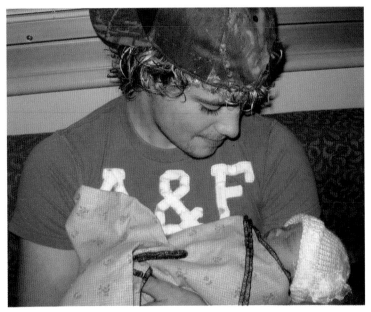

That is just-born Trig Palin. I'm on the sofa in Sarah's hospital suite-delivery room. She was snoozing in the bed next to me, exhausted.

My sister Sadie's sophomore prom night, and a two-month pregnant Bristol, together in my bedroom. This is one of the very few pictures I have of Bristol.

My son, Tripp Easton Mitchell Johnston, being held by Sadie. He is six months old here.

Tripp at two, celebrating Christmas at Grandma Johnston's.

Tripp's bedroom at my house. Just missing one very important person. *Photo by Zach Cordner*

Tank Jones and Rex Butler, doing their best to flank and protect me. *Photo by Zach Cordner*

Bristol, me, Trig, and Sarah. The moment all of our lives changed. I often wish we could go back to the time just before then. *Photo by Paul J. Richards, courtesy of Getty Images*

There is someone in the house, she said.

Wh-a-a-t? I asked. Who? How do you know?

She was frantic, wanted me to get over there fast, to save her and the baby.

Please.

So I slipped a pistol into my waistband and I took Dom with me to drive half-dressed to get to Tripp in record time.

I went raging through the downstairs, past Sarah's two walls of dressers, looked under the king bed, ran past the bathroom's double sinks, and went through Sarah's walk-in closet. Nothing was there. Upstairs, nothing in Willow's room, Piper's, or Track's.

What was that about? Did Bristol want me around, or not?

Every day I spent time wondering what had happened to Bristol to make her change so much. Sure she was a grump when she was pregnant, but always at the end it was, When can we get married? I love you so much.

Early in February, a month after we'd split, Bristol told me that Mommy Sarah had Greta Van Susteren coming all the way to Alaska to interview Bristol and Sarah and Tripp. Bristol was supposed to say she set it up, like she was a big girl. An adult. Her own person. But I could sense Sarah's hand behind that idea.

When the show aired on Fox, I was at Sadie and Mom's.

They wanted to see Tripp. I stood behind the couch and watched with them. On the air, I saw Bristol telling Greta, Levi's a hands-on dad; he's in love with Tripp and sees the child every day.

Right.

Eventually, she said, we'd like to get married.

Hmmm. I wasn't so sure about that idea.

We're both focusing on school now, she told Greta. Bristol wished, though, that Tripp's birth could have happened ten years or so later so that she could have had an education and a job and be, like, prepared and have her own house and stuff.

I wondered if she was remembering how unhappy she was at home and how much she couldn't wait to be out on her own. A big piece of that life-style solution for her was a baby, and me—giving her her own life. It's interesting that it didn't take all that long till her plan pretty much worked. Except for the part about me.

She never mentioned that we were no longer together, or that I'd moved out weeks prior to that. Growing up, she had always been a private soul. Tough to do as Sarah's child, but she still was trying.

Bristol told Greta that having a baby was a load of work. She said she was up all night and it was not glamorous at all. She said she could see herself becoming a spokeswoman against teen pregnancy.

Suddenly, my smiling son appeared on the screen. He was in Mommy Sarah's arms. It'd be the first time the public had a chance to examine my boy. Live! Right after the commercial break.

It was a wonder to watch the next segment, featuring my blue-eyed, blond-haired Tripp. It was also kind of weird to be standing in my mom's house, seeing him on television. It was being filmed only miles away. Sarah explained I was working and going to school. She really had no idea what I was doing, which was remodeling a house with my dad. How could I be going to school?

The show ended with a clip of Sarah strolling out to the river, like it was in her backyard. More bull. The river was the Chena, 197 miles away, a four-hour drive. The Fox people had traveled from Wasilla, set up at the finish line of the Iron Dog, waiting for Todd, the star of the race. That year, for a change, he did not win. It wasn't a winning time all around.

An ABC crew wanting information on Bristol and me corralled me a few days later as I was noodling along in my truck. Someone had leaked the story to the network that we'd broken up weeks earlier, and America seemed to want to know what was going on. The ABC team was hoping I'd spill some dirt about Sarah, pushing me to bad-mouth Bristol, and urging me to complain about not seeing my son.

I had little to say to them.

The coverage, the interest in the Palins—and me—

wasn't over. I'd figured the one good thing that would come from breaking up with Bristol would be that I could at least get my old life back. I figured wrong. After sitting around and stewing for a few weeks, I decided to get out of town, out of range of my cell phone and all other modes of communication. I was going bear baiting. It's like chumming for fish. You throw out bits and pieces of stuff fish like to eat and they begin swimming around in that area. If it's done day after day, week after week, they hang out there, looking for a regular meal. It's bringing your quarry to you rather than trying to find them wherever the hell they are.

I loaded up my truck and headed north.

People have continued to move to Alaska. The state has come a long way from the old gold mining days, and Wasilla had joined in, going through one boom and bust after another.

Wasilla started as a gold-rush town with the 1906 discovery of pay dirt up the road in the Willow Creek Valley. This same thing was happening all over the state.

Prospectors on their way to Nome went by ship. Those coming on foot or by horse, headed for the mountains north of Wasilla, poured into town. Wasilla became a supply and jumping-off point. Main Street started out as the trail to Skyscraper Mountain's Alaska Free Gold Mine, and Granite Mountain's Independence Mine.

Lucky miners flocked back down into Wasilla to cash

out and carouse. Unlucky ones came back into town, their tails between their legs, figured out other ways to make a living, and never left Wasilla.

Alaska is a roundish-squarish giant blob, with two dangling peninsulas at the bottom corners. It looks like my son Tripp's SpongeBob SquarePants toy. Juneau, the capitol, is the kneecap on Bob's left-leg piece of trailing coast—a land fractured by fjords, glaciers, mountains running down to the edge of the sea.

The Aleutian Islands form Bob's other leg that splays to the west.

Anchorage is below, in the crotch.

Wasilla is SpongeBob's bellybutton.

It lays in a valley called Matanuska-Susitna. This Mat-Su Valley is penned in by the Chugach, Talkeetna, and Alaska mountain ranges. Four Alaskan highways go through the Mat-Su. My hometown with a population of seventy-eight hundred, is the valley's biggest community. Even so, it's the fourth largest city in the state. You can drive from my home to half the state's population in an hour.

Everyone lives massed together in a very small piece of Alaska. There is still plenty of empty out there.

It's a big deal in Wasilla when fifteen houses are built. Wasilla is a city but it's a small town in every way. In the lower forty-eight, villages and then towns grow to become cities. In my state, a city can be twenty people; the label has nothing to do with how many live there. Any area that separates from its county, called a borough here, is a city.

The only downtown that Wasilla had was its aging concrete strips of storefronts. New businesses had come in beginning in the late '60s, but since the 1980s, there wasn't much to report. Fleets of black trucks rolled down Parks Highway passing one small plaza after another. If there seemed to be more going on in Wasilla than its population could possibly support, that was because the tiny city was the commerce center of the valley.

We Alaskans had our own way of living. A woman from Biloxi once told me that Alaska is a cold Mississippi. I like to think she was referring to our independent spirit, but she was probably saying we both have our Bubba, our redneck similarities. Laundromats advertise bathroom showers along with washers and dryers. To rent an auto in Alaska, you sign a contract that stipulates "No fish in car." Every third business has *arctic* in its name; the young guys dress in camo wherever the hell they are. In my hometown, our largest food store, Carrs Supermarket, has a sign in its parking lot that says: ABSOLUTELY NO SALE OF PETS ON THESE PREMISES. The number of gun shops is about to be topped by the coffee bistros sprouting up all over town.

The woman from Biloxi was probably right.

I was driving past what we call Alaskan blue daisies—the tarps keeping the snow off rusty beaters, bent lawn furniture, and broken grills. Visitors to the state are so awed by the natural wonders that they often don't notice the downtrodden parts. They don't see this underbelly, the poverty in the margins, away from the cities.

Broke or loaded, every Alaskan shares in the natural glory of the place we live. I see daylight for a few hours in the dark of winter—and sunshine for eighteen hours in the height of summer. I know I'm in Alaska when I walk the woods and after I've hiked all day the distant mountains appear no closer.

That day, as I reached sight of far-off cliffs, I was as close to my final destination as my truck could take me. I pulled over and dropped the tailgate. I lined up the ramps to roll my four-wheeler off the truck bed.

I drove the four-wheeler for two more miles, then pulled over.

With my pack on my back, I began hiking. Already I felt better, cleaner, away from whatever was eating at me back in civilization.

I was restocking the bear bait Dominic and I had hung out there a month before. We had cut a hole in the middle of a fifty-five-gallon metal drum so bears could stick in their heads but not their paws. Within the drum, we had built up a six-inch layer of Ol' Roy kibble, on sale at Walmart, and Wonder bread past its sell-by date. Great Value peanut butter and anise. Bears love the smell of licorice. We had poured a half gallon of vanilla plus blackstrap molasses on top.

The baited oil drum dangled from a pole wedged between two trees, both groaning from the weight. Bears from miles away would come on the scent.

We'd set up a second bear bait on the ground ten yards away. The base was a spread of cheap jelly doughnuts, peanut M&M's—no gummy bears though. We'd piled on jam and marshmallows, Aunt Jemima fake maple syrup, slopping it all together.

We had covered the heap with logs. Bears are as careful as mice. They'll pick around the bait without disturbing the branches. Once they get comfortable, though, they'll toss the logs like impatient teenagers and tear the whole thing apart. That is how you know you've had visitors.

Once a week Dom and I would try to check on the bait, see if we needed to add more goodies. Before we went, we washed our clothes in special no-smell detergent made for hunters. We'd sprinkle our bug dope all around the clearing so the bears wouldn't be worried by a new smell. We wouldn't have lasted ten minutes out there without bug dope.

When we found the bait had been hit, we'd go every other day.

When it rained, it knocked down the smell. I'd sit on my bait pile after a storm, unable to smell a thing. Same goes for the bears. So after storms, we had to rebait.

Our bait was the neighborhood Mickey D's, where bears came for fast food. Once we'd got the bears' attention, if we went dry, it was over. They'd move down the road to the next guy's bait.

It was like my bird feeder at home.

Bear baiting was sort of cheating. It was legal, but wasn't how I liked to do things. It did ensure there'd be a trophy-size bear around for my cousin from New Mexico who'd never hunted, or for other friends who'd flown up from the lower forty-eight. So I did maintain a bear bait, but not on my own. I didn't like to replenish it without Dom or someone else. It was dangerous; the whole purpose of a bait was to attract hungry bears.

But that day I had to do something. I couldn't sit in Wasilla stewing about my Bristol problems any longer.

I spit out my chew before I left the truck; it tended to make me less sharp when I hiked or hunted. It was fine when I fished or played hockey, but not out in the woods. Hunting was even more intense than hockey. In springtime, hungry, thirsty, ornery bears roamed around, fresh out of their hibernating dens. Their fur was thick and pretty, not patchy and rubbed. Later in the season, they started eating fish and began to taste bad.

The state regulated bear hunting. If I shot a bear, I had to report it. I had to show what I'd got. The carcass had to be harvested. Nothing was wasted. No kill for the hell of it.

Bears pretty much followed the same rules.

It wasn't much different from a beef slaughterhouse

that supplied a food market with sirloin, except that in the wild, bears weren't tortured in pens and inhumanely killed.

The bears in the woods were free. Unless, of course, they're careless and get shot.

12

Tank and Rex

I walked along the narrowing trail and sensed my problems with Bristol, and my desire to see Tripp, sneaking back into my head. That had to stop. I was alone and needed to pay special attention. If a bear was behind me and I wasn't on top of the situation, I'd be fucked.

I was getting closer to the bear bait. The goodies were in my giant hunter's backpack. My eyes darted from the trees on one side of the path to the other.

Why did it feel like spiders were crawling around on the back of my neck? I couldn't stand spiders. Now it wasn't only my scruff. My skin felt like I put it on inside out that morning.

I kept moving.

Had I heard twigs breaking? It could have been a squirrel—or a bear. I don't know how they do it, but these massive animals—black bears weigh three times as much as I do—move without making a sound.

Bears are suspicious of bait because it's unnatural. They hunch up, come in slowly, or they hide and wait. If you are in a tree stand and you make any noise or even cough, they aren't going to show their noses.

When we are walking toward a bait, we know bears could be around even if we don't hear or see anything. I've heard the water slushing under their paws, but not them.

I swung to the left and was screwing around with my gun as I glanced to the right where I looked two minutes ago. Now a bear was sitting there, looking at me.

What's up? its expression said. Upon a closer look at its body, however, I began to think the bear wasn't quite as chill as I thought. It had a mass of guard hair all standing on end, stiff like porcupine quills, menacing. I should have brought someone with me to watch my back.

I love bringing folks out to the woods and showing them a good time. That wasn't why I used to hunt, but it is now. My dad was a guide when I was a kid, and when people asked, it's what I used to say I wanted to be. I may still end up in that role. To be a guide in Alaska, you need five years' hunting experience, and I've certainly got that covered. I need to get eight recommendations for the 125 in-field days of work as an assistant guide. I'd also take the registered field-outfitter exam. I'd need to show competency in field procedures. Once I'd been guiding for twelve years with ten recommendations from my clients, I could apply to become a Master Guide.

———

The bear in front of me was in a way assessing my expertise. She still wanted to get at that bait. I snuck a peek and saw a dribble of molasses on the side of her lip. I knew it was a female bear. She wasn't wearing nail polish and didn't have a polka-dot bow on the top of her head, but I could recognize her gender by her fine skull and delicate ears. If I had been in hunting mode, I would have passed her by. The future of Alaska hunting depends on future generations of cubs.

She was standing on her hind legs and sniffing the air. That was her way of tasting me. All of a sudden my backpack with its sugary contents seemed to weigh a ton.

I detected her familiar primal odor.

I was face-to-face with four hundred pounds of grit looming over my own five-foot-ten, 180-pound frame. Despite the name, the black bear isn't always black. They also come in brown and silver-blue. The Europeans who named them only saw the East Coast black-furred ones, so they named them accordingly. The bear looming in front of me made me feel short. I was standing there holding a rifle and I was shaking. It was more than adrenaline; it was life or death.

The bear stamped her foot. I'm a mean critter, she was telling me. You don't want to mess with me, she warned. She snapped her jaw about ten times. Was she nervous, too, or was she doing that to scare me? She was likely hoping I'd turn tail. If the bear saw that she'd won, she would jump on my neck.

I didn't run.

Neither did my friend the bear.

It was a face-off. If she looked at me and I looked at her and we stared at each other for more than two seconds, she would come at me.

Do not stare at this bear, I warned myself.

The creature would do one of three things. She could turn and leave. She could try a bluff charge to break the stalemate: three quick steps and stop, then a circle around to see if I was still there or if she'd successfully scared me off. The third possibility, the worst-case scenario, was that she'd decide to take a fourth full step. She'd come at me full-tilt boogie and attack. If that happened, one of us would be dead.

Not all bears want to attack. Ninety percent of the time, a bear will take off rather than go after someone. The rub is, you can never tell when that 10 percent is going to be.

The bear I was looking at wasn't just standing around scratching her head, wondering what to do with me. She knew. I'd spent more time at Walgreens picking out throat lozenges than she used deciding her next move. She looked like she was having a conversation with the fir tree above my head. That was her level of concern.

The bear barked. Not like a dog, deeper; it rumbled up from her toes.

She glanced at a tree, back at me, then to the tree again. Then she turned and ran up that trunk like a squirrel, not like the cumbersome creature that she was. A minute or two later, I thought I heard snoring. The bear didn't give a shit that I was there. I was insignificant.

Bristol acted the same way. Indifferent. I didn't know if, down the line, some spark would maybe come alive again between us. I hoped for Tripp's sake that we could act decently to each other, maybe even be friends.

Three months after the Greta interview, Bristol was all set up in her own $270,000 condo in Anchorage. She told me she'd paid cash, said she wanted her own place, to do whatever she wanted with Tripp. Sarah had been acting as if he were her son, not Bristol's and, of course, not mine. I was glad his mother wasn't hurting for money.

It's my life, she told me, and my son's.

Actually our son's. I didn't point that out.

My boy moved even farther away from me.

I thought that after we split up, still sharing a son, we could have a simple and easy relationship. If not friendly, at least drama-free. I was wrong. The friction between us continued to grow. And grow. I could feel it in my bones, and I'd be damned if I knew how or why. I was bewildered and caught up in myself, not realizing that people around me were being affected, too.

Since we were little, my sister, Sadie, and I had been joined at the hip. We might be grown-up but we still were close. Bristol either didn't understand or couldn't accept the brother-sister connection. The concept of sharing me with my sister or anyone else was foreign to my babe. I was supposed to focus on Bristol, only Bristol. No Tyson, Dom, Derek, Chad, Mark, Cros—friends I grew up with. And no sister.

There had always been tension between Bristol and Sadie; jealous rage snuck out of Bristol whenever my sister and I goofed around, stuck up for each other. My family had its share of problems, just like everyone else's. Still, we always let one another know that we were there for one another when things were bad. I hug my mom hello; I say, Love you, after talking to my dad, and he says it, too.

It wasn't just Sadie. It was anyone other than Bristol. I think that Bristol's need to be the center of my world was because of her lack of self-confidence, her not-so-positive self-image.

It isn't easy to be the daughter of the beautiful Sarah Palin.

Sarah dressed in clothes that were designed to catch attention; Bristol was the opposite, trying to camouflage her curves. No matter how often I told her that I loved her body, she wasn't comfortable in her own skin. During the time we were together, before she was pregnant, Bristol had had her double chin reduced. I had thought that chin was cute, sort of little-girlish. She still had the liposuction and it seemed to make her happy. Then she decided she needed to get her breasts reduced. It's taken me time and some maturity, though, to get what she had been telling me; that my girls—her boobs—were a physical problem for her. It wasn't just emotional. When she first told me she wanted to have surgery, I was shocked. Her figure was perfect. I got over it though, realized it wasn't about me. It was her body. I supported her. Drove her to appointments, took care of her after the surgeries. I hadn't known liposuction hurt so damn much.

Bristol has had more cosmetic surgery; she showed off her changed features a week before my twenty-first birthday. She told the media about the braces she used to wear. I remember those endless orthodontist's appointments. I never knew it wasn't all taken care of—the alignment issue she pointed out as the reason for her reshaped jaw. I did know she had continued to complain after the lipo about the remaining roundness of her cheeks, a Native Alaskan characteristic that she, Willow, and Piper all inherited from their father's side of the family. And it looks like Tripp, too. To me, it's an Alaskan thing. Bristol looks so different now that it's like she's a new person, but still a looker. I hope she no longer feels insecure about her appearance, although, since she always looked good, I don't think that was the real problem anyway.

———

After Bristol and I had broken up and the fur started to fly, Sadie became my self-appointed protector. She set up a blog and said what she thought. She went crazy when Bristol bad-mouthed my mother. Sadie was angry with the things Sarah seemed to have a need to say about me and my family.

I never read what Sadie blogged, what Bristol blogged. Friends told me. I couldn't stand it. It sounded like a hissy fit to me.

It all had turned me off to the Internet generally. If I opened my laptop, I couldn't seem to check out one thing without all the other shit intruding into my brain.

On Facebook, Bristol was swearing at Sadie, coming out with mean comments. She told Sadie she'd never see her nephew again; she threatened to withhold Tripp from all of us.

Bristol texted Sadie: You r white trash.

When I called Bristol about Tripp, I asked her what the hell was going on. She told me that her mother agreed with everything she was saying. I wasn't surprised. Sarah, stirring up the pot.

The blog vs. Facebook catfight ended when Bristol, who had complete control over the one thing we all cared about, told Sadie online that the Johnstons were no longer allowed to see four-month-old Tripp. I could only have him when Bristol decided it was convenient. My family loved the little guy, and keeping him from us was cruel to all of us, even to Tripp. He may not be able to understand everything around him, but he deserved the love all of us feel for him. Cutting us off was Bristol just being spiteful, caring more about her own feelings than Tripp's right to half of his family, people who cherished him.

The beginning of 2009 had been rough. After I had moved out of Bristol's room, I had tried to not fight with her, to do what she wished so I could see Tripp. All I got was the runaround. It was always the wrong time. Then, if she was aware that I was busy—Wasilla was a small place and we knew the same people—she'd text, You can have Tripp right now. Jerking me around. When I called Bristol to ask what she was trying to do exactly, she said it wasn't her fault. Her mom was acting like my son was her own baby. Sarah didn't want me taking him. I could only see Tripp at their house, I was told, while Sarah and Todd eyed me from the sofa.

We tried that, and it was clear to me that Todd would rather be tuning carburetors. He looked pissed.

I imagined Tripp felt the tension, as two people he knew loved him stared at me like I was the swine flu virus.

Who were these Palins? Why were they so damn mean-spirited?

I had the kind of mind that remembered details. I'd let others run off at the mouth as I recorded it all in my mind's eye. Heartbreaks, hunts, kills, girlfriends, conventions, gigs, loves, lies, dirty tricks, childhood insults, and dreams. Betrayal. Maybe a lot more men are like me than women realize. We hold on to the hurt. Say nothing.

I went along with the craziness for a month or so, until the start of bear season, and that was it. It wasn't healthy for anyone.

Their accusations made for good press. I never came to see my child. I was indifferent. I was a slug. It was Sarah holding the microphone.

While the public took to heart her endless slurs about Levi the absent, uncaring parent, Sarah's Palinbots stopped me on the street and in the grocery to tell me what a son of a bitch I was. Didn't provide for my kid. High school dropout. Trashing the Palins. Why don't you move away? Lowlife. They would knock on my mom's front door, then take off. The calls were endless and late at night; my mom, Sadie, and I all changed our cell numbers. It was offensive, scary to my mom.

Leave my mother alone, you shits.

My mom felt I was the one in need of protection in what was beginning to feel like a public dogfight. Her lawyer suggested that he might be able to help. Maybe, he said, he could straighten things out.

When I met Rex Butler for the first time, it was clear even to this Wasilla boy that this dude cares how he comes across. He's this sharp East Coast guy, in Anchorage, Alaska. He's got his own Rex style. Careful dresser.

Did I believe his real name was Rex Butler? Scarlett's heartthrob. Cosmopolitan Rex from New Jersey told me I wasn't a people person. He noted that I didn't have a lot to say to folks I didn't know. My comfort zone was going out to hunt, he said. I was more relaxed, Rex thought, when I was protected and nobody could get to me. Was that a good thing or a bad thing?

Rex Butler took me on as a client and lined me up with his private investigator, Tank Jones, to help me get some income from all that unwanted notoriety. Tank can be your manager, Rex said. You two will hit it off. He talks a lot; you choose your words. Tank is huge; you're normal. He's black; you're white. He's fifty; you're eighteen. He's urban; you are country.

Oh, yeah, perfect match, I thought. Just like a couple of bookends.

Tank, a native of St. Louis and my guide-to-be in cities, didn't get how my father trained me to find my own way. I'd like to see what would happen if Tank had to put meat—not the store-bought kind—on the table. Who would do better: my bodyguard in the woods for a week or me in St. Louis for seven days?

My pop drilled into me that you can't be an expert at everything. When you're not, find someone who is. For me that was Tank, and Rex.

We all played into my backwoods-boy persona. I was from a small town in an out-of-the-way state. I liked country music. Alan Jackson. Jason Aldean. *Every time you throw dirt on her, you lose a little ground.* I paid attention to George Strait.

I wouldn't, Rex felt, have the confidence to leave Alaska and go on a celebrity trek without Tank. Truth was, I'd traveled a lot on my own, playing hockey.

I needed someone to scout out opportunities, make calls, make it happen. Tank.

He was also my water carrier and protector. When strangers asked how he did that, he suggested they take a step closer and he'd show them. I thought that was meant to be a joke. Tank's as wide as a tree, as gentle as a kitten. A fifty-year-old, six-foot-two-inch black man who has taken a dumb eighteen-year-old under his wing. Tank—he legally changed his first name from Sherman—stepped in when I was about to do something foolish. I only talked to media folks and everyone else when he gave the okay. He saved my white ass every day. He screened my phone calls; he screened my girlfriends, or tried to. He beamed like a proud parent when I acted like I should. He told me I was behaving like a kid when I needed to hear it.

Sometimes he got a little out of hand, but always in a lovable way. So far.

My new cell number and address at my mother's didn't stay secret for long. We couldn't walk out the door without camera lenses focusing in on us. Mom, Sadie, me. Recorders were thrust in our faces. Sadie had trouble leaving the house and getting to school. My mother and sister hung a sign on the door:

IF YOU WANT INFORMATION,
CALL TANK JONES AT 907.444.7194.

Sarah still attacked me and my family whenever she had a chance, so when *GQ* called Tank wanting to profile me, followed by a request from *New York* magazine, I decided to talk. Months down the road, *Vanity Fair* came calling. All three magazines published articles, written from my perspective.

My sister, Sadie, has never been one to stand by and let herself get stepped on. She contacted a show she loved, *The Tyra Banks Show*, asked if they'd like to hear the other side of the Palin story. They responded by flying me, my mother and sister, my pal Cros, and Tank to New York, but that was it—there was no compensation for our appearance.

Before the taping, Tank thought it was a good idea to use this as an opportunity to even the score. I did, too, especially when I thought back to the humiliation of sitting in the Palin living room being observed by Tripp's grandparents, who watched like a couple of vultures from the sofa as I played with my son on the floor.

I was mad. I was indignant. How dare Sarah mess with my ability to be a father to my boy. Who the hell did she think she was?

I'd seen in the Bible that my namesake Levi knew it was wrong to seek vengeance, but he found himself in a situation where he needed to even the score.

That had never been my style.

I tended to do the head-in-the-sand thing. Tried to ignore what was going on and not let things get to me.

It was easy to forgive and forget when the issue wasn't so important.

It was a heavier lift when dealing with inexcusable behavior like the actions of Sarah Palin, my son's grandmother. I knew she loved Tripp with all her heart and I expect him to honor her. But my son needed to respect me as well, to be able to feel good about himself. I feared that if I kept ducking rather than standing up to this woman who demanded two eyes for an eye, the insanity that was my life could continue till kingdom come.

I was about to find out if it was possible to be a forgiving person and at the same time not take anymore crap while Bristol's attorney made filings like this. The bastard.

Ms. Johnston is a convicted felon. She is also a chronic pain patient and undergoes daily, regular, and sustained narcotic infusions. The side effects of such narcotics are well known, but often include sleepiness. The baby cannot be left with Sherry Johnston without someone else there to supervise, as Ms. Johnston could fall asleep or be too drowsy to appropriately monitor the baby. Further, in light of the illegal drug dealing

*by Ms. Johnston, there is a risk that she may re-offend,
keep medications around the house which could be ac-
cessible to the baby, have illegal drug users come to her
house (or she could take the baby in her car during a
drug sale), or otherwise engage in behavior (criminal or
negligent) which could result in a variety of harms to
the baby. For these reasons, any visitation schedule for
Mrs. Johnston should be conditioned on a neutral third
party supervisor, paid for by Ms. Johnston.*

I was counting on Rex to mow down these claims of the
Palin family attorney, Thomas Van Flein, that my loving,
caring family—so much more together than the Palins—
was irresponsible and dangerous. I headed out with Sadie
and Mom, Tank and my childhood friend Cros, hoping to
clear our fucked-up images.

It was a spring day in 2009. Yellow crocuses were
sprouting in planters in front of skyscrapers as the four of
us, and Tank, strolled the streets of New York, relaxing before our appearances on *Larry King, The Tyra Banks Show,*
and *The Early Show.* In our Manhattan hotel the night
before, we had nonstop calls and knocks at our doors.
The paparazzi were on my trail wherever I went, except
my hometown of Wasilla. There, I was the same guy I always was.

Tank went down to the marble-and-gold lobby and
reengineered our check-in info. He came up with fictitious
names for each of us. Tank recalled that Greg on *The Brady*

Bunch changed his name to Ricky Hollywood. So now I'm Ricky Hollywood. My mom is Jessica Brook; Sadie becomes Simpson Shields. All Tank's doing.

Now the paps no longer knew which rooms we are in.

Tank, who sometimes was full of it, carried the charade a step further. He said to me over breakfast the next morning, I just invented an alter ego for you.

I cut him a look, raised my eyebrows. I wasn't buying into it. Forget Ricky Hollywood. We're not going to find my style in the Big Apple.

As we three Johnstons prepared to go onstage on *Tyra*, there was Tank, telling me what to say and what subjects to keep away from. Sarah was fair game.

When I was escorted out onto the set, my heart stopped. They opened the curtain and five hundred people were sitting there. I didn't know there was going to be an audience. It was being taped and I assumed it would just be Tyra. It's me in grade school again, panicked, wondering how I'm going to stand up in front of the class to give my book review. It's me staying home from school, getting a C rather than performing.

When Tyra asked, I said I thought Sarah must have known that Bristol and I were intimate. Moms are smart, I said. I also said again that I lived in the Palin house, had my clothes there. I admitted after some prodding that safe sex wasn't always a top priority. I didn't tell Tyra that Bristol was supposed to be on the pill. I didn't say that Bristol was trying to get pregnant, had wanted her own baby ever since

Trig was born, and even before. I didn't repeat that Bristol had told me her mom wasn't married when she got pregnant with Track, so what was the big deal?

Somehow Sarah saw the tape before it was on the air. She went apeshit. The same day the show ran, she issued a statement, or her hired-gun Meg Stapleton did:

> *Bristol did not even know Levi was going on the show. We're disappointed that Levi and his family, in a quest for fame, attention, and fortune, are engaging in flat-out lies, gross exaggeration, and even distortion of their relationship. Bristol's focus will remain on raising Tripp, completing her education, and advocating abstinence. It is unfortunate that Levi finds it more appealing to exploit his previous relationship with Bristol than to contribute to the well being of the child. Bristol realizes now that she made a mistake in their relationship and is the one taking responsibility for their actions.*

Bristol told me she was as surprised as I was by this statement. But she didn't apologize, didn't say she'd do anything about it, talk to Mommy Sarah for example.

Every day there was endless trash talk about me. Tank was responding, quoting me to all sorts of outlets. I didn't even know what he was dreaming up. I didn't care. My manager knew what he was doing. Let him deal with it all.

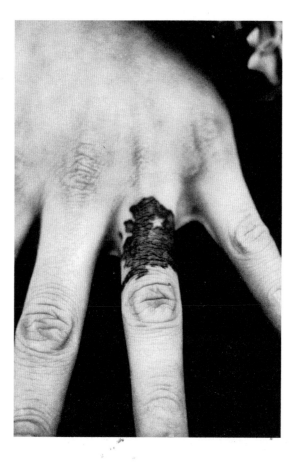

13

Tattoo Redo

The *Tyra Banks* gig was done, and my mom and sister headed back to Wasilla while Tank and I stayed in the city, looking into possible deals, maybe even doing a book. Publishers called him, texted him, e-mailed him.

Now that I was in this crazy world where I might get a gig at any time, it wasn't possible to walk in and get a job at Chepo's Mexican Restaurant on the West Parks Highway in the 'Silla. I never knew when something more lucrative would come up. I had some work at home. My now-divorced dad had married his longtime girlfriend, Lisa, and I worked for her at her processing operation, Pioneer Meats, during the hunting season when she was overloaded with carcasses that needed to be hung, trimmed, and wrapped up for freezers. She mixed up the most delicious moose sticks with cheese, jalapeño, and garlic. I made tasty bear sausage and pepper sticks out of my own kill. When there was too much for everyone I knew to eat, I gave any extra meat to charities. Everyone I knew did that. Why the hell not? It was an Alaska thing.

Other than working at Pioneer Meats and doing odd jobs with my dad, I was looking at the lower forty-eight for income. I knew the outside-Alaska offers were nutty. I knew I was going for it while it lasted. I needed to earn a living.

I survived *Tyra* to go on CBS's *Early Show* with Maggie Rodriguez. I no longer wondered how I was going to react to a live audience. I was over that but still on edge thinking about what I was going to say. We chatted away and I trusted Maggie right off the bat.

I'm not cashing in on the Palin name, I told her. I'm just trying to get my side of the story out there and letting people know who I am. Maggie asked if my heart was broken when Bristol and I broke up. Yeah, I said, it was, and my eyes welled up.

It was Tripp who was in my mind though, not Bristol.

Maybe Bristol a little. The original Bristol.

Unless this was the same Bristol. Unless she hadn't changed and I had.

Sarah, the same old Sarah, was going through some changes herself. I was back in New York when it happened. The producer of CBS's *Inside Edition* had asked me to lace up my skates and play in a league game. I ended up scoring the winning goal in a shoot-out. Right after, someone approached me to ask if I'd heard that Governor Palin was quitting. I wasn't surprised. When I was living in the house, I noticed that her drives back and forth to the governor's office in Anchorage had become less frequent. I hate this job, she used to say. I could be making money instead.

A week after Sarah announced her resignation, I had my BRISTOL finger tattoo reconfigured into the map of Alaska, complete with a North Star. I needed moral support so Sadie, Dom, and another guy, Ben, who has known me since I was a little kid, came along—back to Rebirth Tattoo. Once again, the tattoo artist worked on that sorry ring finger. He didn't have much depth under my skin and it hurt—again—like hell. Alaska is a big state, even if sized to fit around my finger. I remember how I teared up. Dom, the liar, told everyone I was crying like a baby.

The name-tattoo, Sarah the governor, Bristol and I, everything that had been no longer was. It was Alice in Wonderland. My world was topsy-turvy.

I planned to relax and ignore what was going on around me, right after Tank threw a press conference at the office where I gave my take on Sarah's resignation. Time to hit hard, he told me.

I said I thought she wanted to make money. She had talked about doing a reality show, I said, and writing a book. I didn't believe she was resigning because it was best for the state of Alaska. It was going to be best for Sarah Palin and no one else.

She was furious.

Then, two weeks before she stepped down as Alaska's governor, I appeared on the *Today* show. Good buzz, Tank said. This should generate some cash.

Even though everything I said was 100 percent true, Sarah roared like an angry lion. She claimed the liberal networks were backing me. The who?

When I texted about seeing my son, Bristol didn't answer. I knew who would be behind that disregard of our verbal agreement.

My mom told me the press conference and these appearances were dumb publicity stunts and made me look bad. I was being a pawn in adult hands, she said.

Wasn't that what I was saying about Bristol?

The Teen Choice Awards allowed me to at least act my age. It was August and I'd turned nineteen a couple of months before. Now I was in Los Angeles after putting off my caribou and sheep hunting for a week.

The season would open the morning after I was Kathy Griffin's pretend boyfriend for six hours.

I was her escort to the awards ceremony.

Her people had called Rex, my lawyer: We'd like Levi to be Kathy's make-believe lover for the night.

Kathy's huge, Rex told me. This will really help you out. It sounded like fun so Tank and I had flown down to California for the event. After we settled in, Tank wanted to go out for a meal. I hesitated. I can't stand guacamole. I don't like going to California because they put avocados on everything. Even if I told them not to, they did it anyway. California people are weird.

I had no idea what Kathy would be like or what I would be doing, what was expected of me. I'd been told that my gal for the night—Kathy—would fill me in on the way to the venue.

As Tank and I waited out front of the hotel they'd put us up in, there were no Ricky Hollywood–type complications. No paps wanting to photograph me in my pinstripe suit with my pink shirt and matching striped tie.

The year before, if someone had suggested I'd be wearing all this pink shit, I'd have punched them out.

As far as I can tell, no one cared what I had on. In fact no one identified me at all. This might be Hollywood, but Ricky Hollywood was an unknown. Thank God. Afterward, HuffPost did call me Kathy's hunky date.

Awww.

The one person who did of course recognize me was Kathy herself, who pulled up in a white limo that I thought was going to run over our toes before it stopped on a dime.

Kathy threw open the door. She was wearing this lavender gown that looked great. She's my mother's age. My mom is a looker herself.

Now I was sitting next to Kathy, not wanting to wrinkle her dress, which was the color of an Alaskan violet; I got why I was supposed to do pink.

Tank climbed in after me and we were off, headed for the Gibson Amphitheatre in Universal City.

Just be yourself, Kathy said, patting my hand as we rolled along. Act like you're my lover; we'll hug and be affectionate. Let's have fun with this. Fake kissing is good, she instructed.

Then she added, No tongue.

I cracked up.

There were like a hundred celebrities and a herd of photographers and a thousand gawkers. They all ate up our act—smooching, my arm around her, pecking at each other's cheek, and blowing kisses. I kept a straight face—somehow—throughout the whole thing. I told MTV, I don't need to meet anybody; I've got Kathy.

Kathy said, We have a lot in common. We both love hunting.

I knew Kathy does like to hunt Sarah Palin. She called the ex-governor the gift that keeps on giving. Griffin said I'm the silent type who nonetheless gives Sarah Palin the bird when appropriate.

Sarah and Kathy are about the same age, and I found I was as comfortable with this wacky comedian as I had been with Sarah when I used to sit around with her, waiting for Bristol to come home.

Kathy never turned it off. She told everyone, I'm just Levi's trophy girlfriend. She said we had been an item for quite some time but maintaining a long-distance relationship like ours was difficult.

He lives, she told the press, in an igloo and I live in a Hollywood tower.

The event showcased the hottest celebrities, the ones who are the favorites of teens.

The rope line of autograph seekers was waiting about thirty yards down the red carpet. Tank had had me practicing a good autograph signature. He was waiting for me at the end of the line; he wasn't at my elbow to hand me my Sharpie. That was okay. No one asked me to sign anything. Kathy was mobbed. I loved just standing back and watching her do her thing. Again, Sarah's antics when in the spotlight passed through my mind.

Kathy was hands down the funniest person I've ever spent time with. Jokes and one-liners just kept rolling out of her mouth. My stomach hurt at the end of the night from laughing so much.

Kathy said I did fine. Tank said I did great. Maybe I could make my living doing this.

The next year, in 2010, Brittani Senser would ask me to be her date as publicity for the video I would make with her. By that time people knew who I was. A lot happened in between.

After the TCAs, Kathy and I chatted a couple of times. We did *The Joy Behar Show* together, and a year later Kathy traveled to Wasilla to film a segment of her *Life on the D-List* reality show. I was making money as we went ice fishing; I almost lost her assistant through a hole I'd chopped in the lake. Kathy would have fallen off my snow machine if I hadn't caught her; she wasn't holding on like I told her to. This all might have seemed like comedy, but it actually happened. I was going nuts with these tenderfoots.

Then my star decided she ought to give Sarah an invitation to her upcoming *D-List* performance in Anchorage. So she dragged along her camera crew, knocked on the Palins' front door, while I was hunkered down as low as I could get in the backseat of Tank's Navigator. Construction guys—most were buddies of mine—answered the door. They were in there updating the kitchen. The Palins were away. Kathy left the invitation with these meatheads.

My friend Kathy was generous to include me in a number of great gigs. This wasn't one of them. This was dangerous. Was she crazy?

Kathy's birthday is November 4. Her people called Tank asking if I would jump out of a cake for her birthday bash.

Tank was delighted.

I said no way, not if I was expected to do the usual half-nude thing. I loved Kathy and would have liked to be there. But no.

Every so often I had my head screwed on.

This stuff was still new to me and it took me a couple of days to come down from it. I would be almost shaking before; then, once it started, I was okay. I'd come a long way from the kid who would stay home and get a C rather than to have to stand up in front of the class. Still, I was most comfortable up in the woods, and while I was happy to come down to the lower forty-eight for work, Alaska would always be home.

Tank got us lined up for a pistachio commercial. It was Wonderful's Get Crackin' campaign featuring eight celebrities, or so they say. That seemed to include Tank, who was in it with me. They were paying us both, but I didn't know if Tank was one or two of the eight.

Tank had the time of his life. He was laughing and I was laughing at him. The thrust of the filming was my failure to wrap it up. The message was that I now do everything with protection—even eating pistachios. The protection would be my bodyguard Tank. What happened if I didn't do it with protection? That would be Tripp. I wondered what my son would make of this when he was able to understand. I didn't know what to make of it myself.

I'm standing there on set, opening up pistachios. At least I'm totally dressed and I don't see any cakes to jump out of.

They've put me in a pistachio-green T-shirt, with a map of Alaska on the front. Wonderful nuts. That's the brand and they are good. Tank was filmed behind me and off to the side, looking like Tank. It took a day of prep and two days to shoot; Tank had had endless phone conversations with the Wonderful guys to work out the deal.

I get residual checks whenever the ad runs. That was nice but didn't put a dent in the need I had for cash. By the time my manager and my attorney took their cut off the top, there was slim pickings. I was broke.

So we were off looking for more work. Tank and I, along with a new friend of mine, Canaan Rubin, a producer who was talking about a book and reality show package, were back in New York. We're riding down Park Avenue and my cheek was smooshed against the window trying to get a look at this amazing city. The tallest building in Anchorage, the big-mother ConocoPhillips, which sticks up above everything around, is twenty-two stories. I could see to the west the Exxon building, fifty-five stories, when Tank turned and said, out of the blue, If *Playgirl* called you up right now, would you do a photo spread?

Uh, sure. Yeah. I don't know, maybe. I was busy looking at the crowd of people, the lights.

I kept looking up. Now we were passing the Bank of America. Same height as Exxon.

I didn't know what *Playgirl* was. Not really. I knew it was for girls.

Tank said, You know most of the readers are men, right?

I went, So? Didn't bother me. I didn't know what he meant. I didn't know *Playgirl*'s readership was mostly gay guys. I'd never met anyone who I knew was gay. The funny thing was, I was sitting next to my pal Canaan and had no idea he was gay. When I found out, this sheltered boy from Wasilla couldn't believe it. I felt dumb for knowing so little of the world.

Two weeks went by. Canaan was back in L.A. and I was in Wasilla. When we were in Alaska, Tank Jones, my traveling buddy, morphed back into a private investigator, working out of Rex's law offices.

One morning Tank called and he went, Hey, still want to do *Playgirl*?

Why?

They want you.

I got into my truck and drove the highway from Wasilla toward Anchorage, passing by the Mercedes-Benz dealership, Old Navy, the Anchorage Museum in downtown. In less than an hour, I was parked in the lot behind Rex's office. I walked into the building and stepped into the elevator. Tank was waiting for me on the third floor, right inside the door—back against a wall of matted press clippings and thank-you's from Rex's clients, all framed.

Tank stopped leaning. He had this centerfold hanging out of his hand in front of a blooming poinsettia.

They want to do hard copy, he said. Although they haven't printed a magazine in years—it had been all online—now they want to feature you in their return to print.

I looked at the centerfold guy. I wasn't liking this.

I needed the cash.

I ended up going for it.

Playgirl announced I would be in the magazine. It was a big splash, then they suggested that I needed to do what actors do. Get in the gym. I thought, The heaviest thing

I've lifted in months is Tripp's car seat. Tank signed me up with his brother Marvin, a former Mr. Alaska contender, who now became my bodybuilding coach.

I started working out in Marvin's gym in Anchorage. He made Tank look like a schoolgirl. The guy was an animal, a big bonehead, and I meant that. Like Tank, his head was shaved so you could see the shape of his skull. Both brothers should have been named Tank. Number One and Number Two.

Marvin got me at it two hours a day, six days a week. I wanted to look like the guy working out next to me. His back muscles rippled like minnows in the water.

Marvin's workouts were hard and boring as hell so I asked friends to join me, a different one each time because no one ever came back. I brought Dane, one of my old high school buddies. He played hockey with me. He ended up puking three minutes into it, and went home.

My pal Ben almost stuck it out, but he got really sick. It was just all bad for Ben. He couldn't finish.

He came back a week later and ended up puking and leaving.

Marvin didn't allow time to go to the bathroom to heave. I used the bucket alongside the bench. Marvin did give me time to wipe my mouth.

The one guy who stuck with the whole routine was Dom. He was my height, lean, but every pound of him was muscle. A well-built guy with Popeye arms. He loved the workout. I love him. He's the pussy of my group of friends. No, don't do that, he'll say when somebody has dreamed up some crazy shit. We did it anyway, and then we were sorry.

The shoot was coming up; Tank set up for me yet another appearance with Maggie Rodriguez on *The Early Show*. As always, I counted on him to tell me what I should say, but I wanted to speak out more, express my frustration about not seeing Tripp enough:

I'm here to try to tell my side of the story; I'm unable to see my boy. Sarah is powerful and has destroyed my reputation, and then she uses that as a public reason for denying me access to my child. Her attorney repeats her statements as if they are facts on court documents.

Tank wanted me to convey the message that if the Palin troops continued to go down this road, they'd better watch out because he kept a list of the bad things I knew and had mentioned to him. I wasn't going to go that far. I realized that he kept no such record; when I asked for it, he never showed it to me.

If I really wanted to hurt Sarah, I could—easily. I did say that. So I guess I did go that far. In fact, I went way beyond where I should have.

I said that Sarah called Trig her little retard. It wasn't that one time that she did it and then winked at me. It happened more than once. Her kids were used to hearing it. I didn't know if they felt the way I did, and I wasn't as

clear with Maggie as I should have been—that Sarah wasn't
saying anything in a cruel way. She wasn't saying, You are
retarded. She was just kidding around with her family. Oh,
a retarded baby. She was joking around, at the same time
maybe wanting to pick up Tripp because he was more fun,
better able to respond.

Still, it was unkind.

I must have hit a nerve. Sarah's reply on CBS the next
day questioned the credibility of someone who was going
to bare all for *Playgirl*. Consider the source, she said, of the
most recent attention-getting lies. Those who would sell
their body for money reflect a desperate need for attention
and are likely to say and do anything for even more attention.

I had told Tank I wasn't posing naked for any magazine. No
frontal nudity. I thought *Playgirl* was the female equivalent
of *Playboy*. I'd read *Playboy*; I had friends who bought it.
Classy articles and recipes I wouldn't touch. I should've
realized the deal when, back in my hometown, I tried to
buy the magazine. I couldn't find it anywhere. All I heard
was the thud of $50,000 being dropped into my empty
bank account. That was a huge amount of cash, and Tank
assured me that the spread would be a class act. Besides,
I would be following in the footsteps of Brad Pitt, Mario
Lopez, Jim Brown, Nicole Kidman's husband Keith Urban,
wrestler Shawn Michaels, and even old Burt Reynolds.

That made me feel better about what I was going to do for a New York minute maybe, or a Wasilla second.

There'll be a video of my shoot. It'll go viral, Tank told me. Gay guys will love it.

What the hell was I thinking?

Doing *Playgirl* gave Sarah an opening. I was the same guy she used to bear-hug and wink at, acting like I was her son, like she loved me. Now she told the press, anyone who would listen, it was disgusting that Levi's going to pose for porn.

I had to laugh. This is someone who'd arrange herself on a bearskin rug whistling through her flute for enough cash. There's a reason there's a Photoshop'd picture of her all over the Net—in a red, white, and blue glittery bikini, clutching a rifle. She was a beauty queen, Miss Wasilla, 1984.

Sarah was a good-looking woman who would peek from under her lashes to make sure she'd been noticed. She thought it clever when her gaggle of girlfriends, the Elite Six, had bent and stretched for an exercise exhibition at the Alaska State Fair in exchange for parking and food. The women pulled the men away from the giant pumpkin exhibit around the corner. Sarah knew exactly why those guys at the fair lined up to watch.

I was making excuses, but I didn't see much difference between a Miss Alaska contest and a *Playgirl* shoot, and even politics. I did have to admit that, when my beautiful sister, Sadie, posed for a *Playboy* centerfold, I was grumpy. But she was my little sister and I loved her. Like me, she was told there would be no frontal nudity there either.

I'd watched Sarah, looking like a normal Wasilla mom, all of a sudden kick it up and turn it on. She'd prime herself, get mentally ready. Stop; stand up straight; smile. Then walk out to her car waggling her index finger as she talked to herself.

She told me this story about the time she'd decided to get the votes of the Wasilla councilmen by wearing a push-up bra under a see-through blouse that showed, as my mom would say, a lot of throat. Sarah laughed as she remembered this episode, ignoring her husband, Todd's, face, not noticing as his ice-blue eyes shut down.

That same Sarah with the toothpaste smile and the snappy glasses told me her base in the national election was young males. She liked that; attractive women do. If a man whistled at her as she walked by, she'd wave back.

I was an inexperienced kid when Sarah, loaded with charm, gave me a window into the workings of her kind of female. Maybe, with the upcoming *Playgirl* photo shoot, I would be toying with the masculine version of those moves myself. That thought wasn't comfortable.

14

The Reveal

Sixty days later I flew into Newark, New Jersey, for *Playgirl*. A crowd of teenage girls was waiting for me. Me! Well, maybe a half dozen. They were off to the side and I almost missed them. One held up a sign that said HIGH SCHOOL HUNK. I learned what speechless meant. I had no words. I had no idea how these kids knew I was arriving, and why they'd shown up for me.

I asked Tank, who said he had no idea, but smiled a lot.

Playgirl staff had come out to greet me as well. One dude took us and our bags to a big, white van covered with *Playgirl* lettering and photos of near-naked guys, careful to not show their junk. Tank laughed his ass off. I told the guy, I'm not riding in that van. He put me in a town car.

All I cared about was getting the shoot done before I lost my muscles. I was sticking to Marvin's low-carb, high-protein diet until I got through here.

This exposure, Tank told me, might jump-start an acting career if I had what it took. Then again, he added, modeling might be a better route.

I said nothing. What for? It was just talk. I might end up doing anything, anywhere. As the elevator took us up to the studio, I told myself that this shoot was a part of a new life plan, that I was in control. Deep down I knew I was on autopilot, not navigating at all, doing what the adults told me to do. I could end up anywhere, all the while telling myself this was what I had planned.

On a floor overlooking Second Avenue, I sat on a high stool, drinking a bottle of water as they arranged the shoot's setup. I was in a robe with PLAYGIRL embroidered on the chest. I had no idea that, when my issue hit the stands, I'd get credit for reviving the publication's dying brand. Subscriptions went through the roof.

Right then, I was just an edgy nineteen-year-old kid.

Okay, Levi, we're all set up. Let's start out with your looking right at me. Great. Hold it. Nice.

I hoped to come across as cool as a cardsharp.

Could you roll over, please?

I felt like an idiot. Levi Johnston, the stooge, flat on his stomach with his cheeks in the air.

My mood changed. Now I'm thinking, What will my son say when he's all grown-up and sees this spread?

Sarah's right. It is sleaze.

John, can you pat Levi dry please. He's perspiring.

Damn right I am. It was like my scalp was on fire.

A guy a little older than me trotted over with a piece of cotton to pat my chest—I didn't need a wax because I have no chest hair. John looked me in the eye and smiled as he dabbed at the sweat pooling in my navel.

Tank had told me to expect this. You're going to meet all different types of people, he said. Don't overreact. Nobody's gonna hurt you. I'll be there.

Hey, Levi, one of the *Playgirl* staff asked. How about trying on this fedora? You'll look like Matt Bomer, from *White Collar*.

I'd never heard of Matt Bomer. That night I checked out *White Collar* and Matt online in the hotel. I would buy a fedora before leaving town.

Peter, fix Levi's hair. I want a curl to come down over his forehead . . . no, no, the other side. . . .

On your back, please, left knee up. Excellent.

I performed as I was told, but I was sure my face changed color as often as the ten traffic lights we have back in the 'Silla.

Oh, no, someone said. His ass wasn't waxed. They seemed to have wanted my rear end to be as smooth as Tripp's. The day before I had called a halt when they had started fussing with my eyebrows, and they must have gotten distracted away from my butt.

Now roll over on your left side and pull up your right knee. Janice, grab that towel.

In a minute a hockey glove was all that kept me from

nakedness in front of a crowd of strobe lights and people staring at me. I continued to hold the line at full frontal nudity for the cameras. I had no idea what the plan was with the hockey stick in the corner.

Good, good . . .

That's it, Levi, the photographer said. The strobes were switched off.

Great job. It's a wrap.

I didn't think so. Pulling my pants up in the *Playgirl* dressing room, it hit me. I had no idea what I was doing and I didn't have much time to worry about it.

After I finished *Playgirl*, I felt like I'd just climbed the Wrangells. Was Sarah right? Was I a bloodsucking tick, living off her fame? Was I lost? Worse, was I a shitty dad?

Those thoughts hit me hard as we headed for Alaska.

Back home in Wasilla, I went into hibernation. I stopped reading papers, magazines, and let the e-mails pile up on my server. The one time I went online, I found my name generated more than a million hits. When I couldn't seem to fall asleep, I watched hunting videos all night long.

I had learned little about life and how to deal with it. I was unprepared for what might be lurking outside my front door. I was like my dad's late friend, the bow hunter.

This pal of my father's went into the woods alone to re-plenish his bear bait. He was looking around and enjoying the scenery. He didn't see this bear lying behind the pile, fast asleep, hidden in the shade of some trees.

The hunter stooped to add bait and woke up the bear. It was game over.

The bear ate the bow hunter's ass real quick.

All my dad's friend had was a bow strapped on his back, out of reach. Since hearing this story—how the hell does my dad know what happened?—I now have a harness for my bow, and I carry my rifle in my free hand.

That's how I see Rex and Tank. My weapons at ready in my right hand. I'd be naked without them.

So why did I feel like someone was chewing up my ass?

A few days later, Rex, Tank, and I flew to L.A. *GQ* had done a profile on me so they invited me to their Man of the Year Awards. And Tank. When Tank and I stood in line waiting for our turn to walk the red carpet, I noticed I was standing right behind Kim Kardashian. What a great ass. Tank had to nudge me. I turned to him and saw that Mr. Clint Eastwood was behind me.

A Radar Online reporter asked about my *Playgirl* shoot. No, there was no frontal nudity. No, I wasn't doing another shoot; once was enough. I told him my sister had just laughed at the early pics and that I had not yet gotten a reaction from my old man, and I hoped I didn't. I didn't add that I already knew that Sadie would be doing her own "Girls in the Ice" or some such shit for *Playboy.*

The reporter walked away to chat up the real stars who were there. I was not Mr. Clint Eastwood. I wasn't even Kim's ass. No one reacted to me, or to Tank. It was a bit of a downer.

Rex and Tank grazed the buffet while I looked for a Dr Pepper. The Hollywood crowd didn't do Dr Pepper. Little knots of people, like nonbettors at a craps table, were circling the celebelitists. Kobe Bryant, Lindsay Lohan. Morgan Freeman. I was left alone.

The three of us left in an hour. It turned out I didn't need one bodyguard, much less two.

I could have used some reputation protection a week later, though, as Sarah went on *The Oprah Winfrey Show* as part of her publisher's book tour. While she was there to pitch *Going Rogue*, she spoke of me as well.

I don't know if we call him Levi, she said with a cute tilt of her head. I hear he goes by the name Ricky Hollywood. So, if that's the case, we don't want to mess up this gig he's got going. Kind of this aspiring . . . porn . . . The things that he's doing; it's kind of heartbreaking.

Bringing up Tank's Ricky nonsense, from back when I was looking for my personality. Ricky Hollywood. It does sound like a teenage stripper—with his giant sidekick named Tank Jones. Tank's the biggest in an avalanche of T-names that includes my son, Tripp; Trig, the youngest Palin; Sarah's spouse, Todd; their firstborn, Track. What was I thinking when I named my cat Trigger?

Sarah didn't want to let it go. Poor Levi; he's lost.

Well, maybe.

If only Sarah had known what was lurking in the wings. At the same time she was trashing me, Rex was talking to Corbin Fisher, who proposed I get into the movie business. Actually, the gay porn section of the film industry. Fisher wrote Rex a letter offering me $100,000 to film three masturbation scenes. I was trying to understand how the conversation went beyond the first phone call. That was horrible.

Thank God Sarah didn't know about this when, still on *Oprah*, she changed directions to take another shot. Just in case some of *Oprah*'s viewers missed the comments she had made on CBS three weeks earlier, she repeated that the father of her grandson was a porn star.

All this without having seen the not-yet-published spread. No frontal nudity, damn it. Does that make it okay?

Three days later, things clearly were not okay. My mom was finally sentenced. I almost jumped over the courtroom railing. With no prior record, she was nonetheless hammered with jail time. It was the craziest, most insane thing that has ever happened to any member of our family. Mom, sick as a dog but tough as nails at the same time, went back to jail for twelve months, until she was released on medical consideration and given home probation with an anklet. It was the worst experience of my life. Hers was worse. I worried about her night and day and so did my sister. Our extended family was there for mom, supporting her and visiting her in jail. Still, it was hell.

Within a month, my wrath switched from criminal to family law, all in the same Palmer courthouse. Rex had represented Mom; now I was his client.

Bristol is, or at least used to be, a decent person. I had almost married her. Now, with unlimited cash and her mom's legal eagle standing ready, she had filed stacks of complaints in Family Court. When I asked her what the hell she was doing, I didn't recognize that Bristol was parroting me when she blamed it all on Sarah's attorney. Oh, Levi, you know I don't understand it. It was like me saying to myself that Rex deals with it; I'm paying him to keep track and I don't need to follow things.

Bristol told me, as a general remark was filed about me, that it was just legal stuff. Oh, Levi, you know it doesn't mean anything. Sarah's lawyer says we have to do this stuff.

The evidence will show that Levi is not ready for the demands of parenthood and the sacrifices that would entail to a 19 year old aspiring actor/model. Levi remains without a regular job or steady source of income. He has obtained money by selling stories to the media about his son Tripp, ex-fiance Bristol and the Palin family in general, but otherwise has not gone to school to learn a trade or obtain a degree. Recently he has

engaged in modeling, including risque modeling for
Playgirl *magazine.*

Bristol had claimed I was in contempt for not comply-
ing with a gag order? The judge saw it my way. Bristol
requested I pay her legal fees? Denied. She said I owed support back to the time of birth, when I already was supporting Tripp? Nope. Sarah moved to close the proceedings so
Bristol and I could hide out as John and Jane Doe? Not if I
was expected to survive, I told the court in so many words:

*I do not feel protected against Sarah Palin in a closed
proceeding. I hope that if its open, she will stay out of
it. . . . I think a public case might go a long way in
reducing Sarah Palin's instinct to attack and allow the
real parties in this litigation, Bristol and I, to work
things out a lot more peacefully than we could if there is
anymore meddling from Sarah Palin. . . .*

*I know that public scrutiny will simplify this mat-
ter and act as a check against anyone's need to be overly
vindictive, aggressive or malicious, not that Bristol
would ever be that way . . . but her mother is powerful,
politically ambitious and has a reputation for being
extremely vindictive. So, I think a public case might go
a long way in reducing Sarah Palin's instinct to attack.*

The judge went my way, but so what? We won these
small battles, but not the war. Rex said the Palin plan was

to overwhelm me with legal challenges until I was broke. It was working. We still had no signed agreement on custody or visitation. No court order ended up meaning no Tripp with his pop.

When Rex explained to me the next day that $300 of my monthly money was targeted for health insurance for Tripp, who didn't need it, I didn't want to hear it. I didn't care if I paid when he already had medical coverage through a free federal health program. His grandpa Todd is part Native Alaskan, a Yupik. This allowed Bristol and Tripp, also considered to be Yupik, to enroll as members of the Curyung Tribal Council, within the Bristol Bay Native Association consortium. They could get care through the Indian Health Service. The Alaska Native Medical Center was free to Tripp.

I didn't follow what Rex was telling me. I didn't give a damn and didn't want to be involved in any of this crap. I had never even stepped foot in Family Court. Rex said I didn't need to be there, although one time I heard there was all sorts of flack about how I was supposed to show up and had not.

Let Rex deal with it. Let him answer Bristol's bullshit claims that I paid child support only now and then. Bristol didn't cash my checks—giving her the ability in her mind to say I wasn't supporting Tripp.

The Palins didn't let me have time with Tripp, then claimed I'd not seen him for months. They were working both sides of the street.

Let Rex reply to filings for full custody of Tripp.

I'm more comfortable above it all—in a tree stand, looking down.

Tripp turned one. My son's December birthday came and went without my participation. The Palins had a nice party for him. I wish I had been there but that's okay. It was great to see the published photos. Tripp looked so happy and I was delighted.

We Johnstons had our own happy event a month late, in January. I had asked my friend Canaan Rubin, a producer-director, for advice. How, I said, do I preserve my son's first birthday? With Sadie's camera, or should I get someone to shoot a video? The always-thinking Canaan said he'd fly up and tape it for *Entertainment Tonight*. So Tripp's second first-birthday party at my mom and Sadie's place would become a big deal—and lots of fun. I was in a terrific mood looking forward to the big day.

Bristol had called the week before to tell me that Tripp had said my name. Dad. Of course, said Bristol, he knew exactly who he was talking about.

Bristol and I were beginning to do okay discussing Tripp, and that was what was important. She and I, and Tripp, too, had dinner in Anchorage one night. We talked mostly about our son, then took a walk and bought ice cream. I thought that Tripp looked more like me than he had when he was younger. Everyone said that. Bristol laughed.

Bristol had said it would work for her to let me have Tripp on Wednesdays and Saturdays. Wonderful. It would be on a Wednesday that my son smeared cake all over himself. I was pumped that I would now get to see him twice a week. I didn't want to dwell on what had happened in the past.

The next month, after a year of endless crap about how I wasn't seeing and taking care of my son, a poll came out that showed I was the most hated man in Alaska. I remembered that Sarah, when she was governor, had some sort of sneaky system to rig polling. I didn't even think she had to do that here. The negative info smeared all over the Internet and TV had worked its magic, and continued to spread and do damage.

Mom was walking around Lake Lucille, at the Best Western that's about four hundred yards from the Palins'. There's a peaceful patch of grass and a gazebo that she liked to sit in, enjoying the view of the mountains backdropping the lake. Three anonymous tipsters called the police claiming she was attempting to approach the Palins, or Tripp, or someone. Her probation officer barred her from that area of town.

Bristol and I finally had a court order from the judge about child support. My lawyer conceded that I'd earned more than $100,000 in 2009. The top amount Alaska could require one to pay for one child was $1,750 a month. That would be my obligation until I asked that it be revisited. Rex wrote a $21,000 check against my account to Bristol for child support. I was useless and unemployed— except when they were calculating my income—and Tripp wouldn't be safe with me or my mom. I guessed that I was all things at all times to the Palins and Mr. Van Flein.

Bristol, different things at different times herself, was about to be a starlet, acting as an unwed mom in the TV show *Secret Life of the American Teenager.* That was in March, when she also taped a public service announcement to air in May for National Teen Pregnancy Prevention Month.

The month before, in April, Samantha Harris had asked me on *Entertainment Tonight* to share with her audience what I thought of Bristol's PSA. As Samantha rolled it, I saw that Bristol held Tripp on her lap and explained over his head how hard he made her life. I scratched my head, trying to understand how this was a pro-life message. With abstinence thrown in. I didn't know what the hell to think.

That wasn't what I said to Samantha. I told her that Bristol was making a good point.

I know when I have Tripp, it is tough, I said. I have to keep an eye on the little guy every minute. But, I explained, it's not about me. I wouldn't go back and change it for anything. He's the best thing that's ever happened to me, so I'm sure Bristol's thinking the same thing.

She must be.

I always tried to make everything sound as good as possible, hoping it might turn out to be true. I'd been seeing Tripp at least once a week and things, I explained to Samantha, were good as long as I played by his mom's rules. I was willing to do that. I've had it with the fights. I'm not sure I realized that I'd lost a day a week of visitation along the way. Bristol would drag the baby along to go shopping when it would have been easier to go alone. Yet, she wouldn't let me have him instead. I would never take Tripp from Bristol. She's his mom and that would be cruel. Wait a minute. That's what Bristol had already tried to do to me. Sole custody—and that's what she was doing whenever she wouldn't let me have Tripp on my days.

She wasn't the kind of girl to even come up with this stuff. Sarah was using her political skills on her daughter. Willow could resist Sarah's manipulations, but Bristol was a pushover when it came to dealing with Mommy Sarah.

All along my female friends had been trying to convince me that Sarah had had a cougar crush on me and was jealous of Bristol once we had a child together. They had me watch *The Graduate*. I'd seen it before, but hadn't paid it any mind. They thought I should and explained it to me as it went along. Like I couldn't get it myself. Sarah was Mrs. Robinson and I was her Benjamin, with Bristol the ever-hopeful bride Elaine. Mr. Robinson, Todd, was in there, too. Both he and his wife were out for Benjamin's blood when he ran off with Elaine.

DEER IN THE HEADLIGHTS

It's a classic situation, my female friends told me, while their menfolk rolled around the floor cracking up.

What did come to mind was how Sarah behaved with men her own age. I remember her standing next to my dad in the stands in the hockey rink in Fairbanks, rubbing the back of his neck. He wasn't the only guy she was flirty with. I thought my mother would have a stroke. What could she say? Get your paws off my property?

Sarah could care less as she linked arms with another father and walked away. It was her mojo, her strength. Her sexuality. It was pretty powerful.

15

The Trickster Strikes Again

I didn't want to get into that older-woman/ younger-guy Freudian shit. I just wanted to see my kid, that's all, and care for him.

I also wanted the trash-talking about me and my family to stop. I'd given up on any relationship with my favorite Palins, like Piper. And Sarah's father, Chuck Heath, who might not have known what was going on when he told the press that I ought to be buying diapers for the baby. I was and had been since the day he was born. His comment stung. Both Chuck and his wife, Sally, were always nice to me. They told me I was their definition of the Alaskan boy; I had English setters; I was a big-time fisherman and loved hunting. My teen chest swelled a little when they told me that.

How had it happened that our mutual affection was smothered by anger? How did meanings get so twisted that you couldn't even recognize the original thought? What causes love to turn into hate? Does someone have to do something to make that happen? For me, yes, someone does.

Rather than dwell on all this, I worked at filling the space between my ears with nothing—white noise, referring everyone to Rex and Tank, who kept my calendar. I hid out beneath my Camo Seclusion comforter, licking my wounds. I stayed in bed in the mornings as long as I could.

I uncoiled once in a while. I forced myself to play adult hockey. I joined what was nicknamed the Beer League— a senior's group where older guys had a brew and then played, then had a couple more. I wasn't old enough to drink. I needed my wits about me anyway. These games were fast-paced. One guy had played for the Alaska Aces. Semipro. There were ex–junior hockey players. There were Division I college players. I wasn't the best player, but I could hold my own.

I caught a weekend game. It felt good to be back on the ice.

Slowly I began to accept, as I had to. At first, I hated the idea of a world without Bristol and Tripp. Little by little I started to face facts. I still wasn't realizing that, no matter who was handling my life, I had to pay attention. I might have had my hands free so I could carry a gun with my bow on my back—but I still needed to make decisions. Only I knew when it was time to act, to move.

I would learn that.

I didn't know it yet.

———

Harper's Bazaar did a shoot for Trig's birthday. *Harper's* staff dressed the whole family—except Todd, who didn't participate. Willow and her cousin Lauden babysat Trig and Tripp during the shoot.

I hadn't seen Trig—my special little boy—for so long and would love to have been included. I had to settle for the magazine version. The Palins all looked great.

Too bad Bristol lived in a not-so-great area. I noticed when I picked Tripp up that the neighborhood was kind of ratty. I couldn't imagine why Sarah and Todd had wanted their daughter and their grandson in that sketchy location, but maybe I was overprotective.

If I were to walk Tripp around there, I'd feel like I needed to take my gun. One sunny spring afternoon, Bristol and I did take Tripp for a stroll and talked about our son. God, it was wonderful. That court appearance over cash seemed to have cleared the air. Or maybe it was that it was just the three of us. Not Rex or Tank, not Sarah or Van Flein. No adults sticking their noses in, having their own agendas.

The next morning I crawled out from under my camo blanket—and then bam! My heart rate was turned up a few notches.

How R U? Bristol texted.

I couldn't help it. I typed back, I miss U Bristol.

Bristol answered, I love U. I want to B with U again.

Thank goodness those texts were private, unlike those

we used to exchange in high school. Back then, Todd called my mom in a rage. He asked her what she was going to do about the texts her son and Bristol were exchanging. Bristol talked trash far worse than I did, even in texts. Mom asked Todd how he knew what we were writing to each other. Did he pry into his children's cell phones when they left them lying around? And what exactly was he doing about Bristol's texting?

Like Willow, Todd liked to keep tabs, catch people doing stuff they shouldn't.

He had also called Mom looking for Bristol on those nights when she told her parents she'd be at a friend's and instead stayed with me, at home or in the woods.

Other than that, he was aloof.

Mom thought Todd was an arrogant ass.

A month later, in June, I sat in my living room and watched my babe on *Good Morning America*. She explained how she and I were coparenting and how good that was for Tripp, who was there with her, on the air. The two of them looked like a perfect portrait of my little family.

Within a few weeks, Bristol and I were more than coparenting. We were together, in her condo.

Bristol had moved into the unit the year before—gone from the house she grew up in, for the first time in her life. She told me she had been as excited as any new homeowner would be. She had run around buying furniture, lamps, sheets, a rug.

She also bought pots and pans. This was a good idea. She was the only Palin who could cook. Actually Sarah did make one meal I can remember, for my eighteenth birthday. I was floored. She had sent one of the kids out for some fast food, and we ate that along with the moose tacos she was laying out. She had even invited my mom and Sadie. They and Bristol and I ate on the sofa; I balanced Trig on my knee while I forked in the grub. Todd was outside and Sarah disappeared into her room with a dish of food. The girls were upstairs. I did think it was sweet of Sarah, a real gesture.

Little did Sarah know that night that Bristol had something other than moose meat in her tummy, and that her daughter, Bristol's friend Sammy, and I would be bringing her and Todd up to speed that next day. My mom had felt uncomfortable being over there knowing our secret—and knowing that the other set of parents did not.

It was more than two years since that moose-meat night; I had had two more birthdays, and Bristol and Tripp had been settled into the Anchorage condo on Turnagain Street, with its three bedrooms and two baths. Willow, fifteen, would stay over and, sometimes, Track's girlfriend since seventh grade, Britta Hanson. Bristol, who had

always been afraid of the dark, liked the security of somebody else sharing her and Tripp's space.

Tripp had his own little bed in his own bedroom.

It seemed to Bristol and me that it was our turn again on
Turnagain Street. I saw that as an omen. Sure, a part of
me was gun-shy, but I was so happy to be with Tripp that
I ignored any lingering worrisome thoughts. This was the
point when I should have—but didn't—recall the lesson of
my father and one not-quite-clever-enough bear.

Dad was tending a bear bait. One day when he found
his pile trashed, he rebaited it and, from then on, started
visiting it every day, planning to get his bear. Every time
he checked, the bait pile was devoured, but Dad could
never spot the culprit doing it. He couldn't understand
it—where was the damn bear? My father decided to stay in
the woods up in a tree all night, trying to figure out what
was going on. Still no bear.

In frustration, Dad asked a friend to come with him.
They walked in together, making plenty of noise. At the
bear bait, my father snuck up a tree while his buddy re-
filled the bait and left. Fifteen minutes later, there was the
bear, creeping along, going for the pile of bait.

Dad figured it had been sitting and watching, waiting
until the coast was clear so he could enjoy an easy sweet
meal.

They get smarter and smarter, these bears, but not

smart enough. This was one of the biggest my dad ever shot. If the bear had realized that things change and you need to keep an eye out for that possibility, he'd still be out in the woods.

Like the bear my dad shot, I was acting on what I assumed to be true and wanted to be true. The bear knew my dad's pattern and wasn't thinking anything could be different. I felt that Bristol's love text was wonderful news; that we'd get together again and be as close as we were back in high school. I moved quickly, without thinking. I should have considered what Bristol might now be doing—and Sarah, too—and not have assumed that we would go back to where we were when we were in love.

At first it was like old times when we played our song, Nickelback's "Far Away." Back then, and still now, I sucked in the smell of her perfume, Viva La Juicy, and was swept away. La Juicy was a part of my oxygen supply even for the year and a half we were apart.

Now, though, we weren't apart. Far from it. At night, when Tripp crawled in with us, I would feel light-headed, dizzy with pleasure. We cuddled our little guy between us, and I let myself believe it was forever.

I still wasn't all the way comfy, though, as I had been when I was living in the Palin house. Sometimes I'd get thinking and would get scared, like it could end and I'd be apart from Tripp again. When I felt that way, I considered bringing over my camo quilt and my camo slippers, but decided against it.

I was good.

I was thinking it would be the time for me to get to work on finishing high school. Bristol had. She started a high school correspondence course through some church group during what would have been her senior year, but whether she submitted her work or not, she said her mom had it set up that she'd get a degree from Wasilla High. She had first gone to Wasilla High; then transferred to Juneau's high school; and finally was a student at West High in Anchorage when she got pregnant. For the remainder of that school year, she was signed up for this church program. Then, at the end of her senior year, she got a diploma from Wasilla High. Which was great.

I had dropped out my junior year two months before it ended, to work. So I still had a year and a half to go. I needed to look into taking the GED exam.

The important things in Bristol's schedule that summer of 2010 were her speaking engagements. Although Sarah never lectured Bristol on the subject or even mentioned it, my babe had now been transformed into a sexual-abstinence advocate.

I told her it sounded sexy dirty to me. Bristol had her head on my chest when I said that and just started to laugh in that way she had. I couldn't help it, I ended up joining in. We were both doubled over. She was trying to tell me something and couldn't get it out because she was giggling so hard. I propped her up so she could get out what was so funny. She caught her breath enough to tell me that, when her mom first mentioned this career possibility to her, Bristol asked her what abstinence was.

She was just joshing me, making fun. She was collecting piles of money describing the horrors of teen pregnancies and before that, of course, teen sex. Which every single kid Bristol and I knew was engaged in. Give me a break.

She showed me the Candie's shoes. There were these bamboo jobs; others had silver zebra skin. These were the kind of shoes that announce, I'm here and I'm hot. Wow, I said over and over. Candie's is a perfect company for you to hook up with, I told her. Those shoes should come with a black-box warning.

Bristol had her shoe slogans memorized: *If I can prevent even one girl from getting pregnant, I will feel a sense of accomplishment* and *Pause before you play.* We talked about abstinence, if it would have been better if Tripp were born several years down the road. He was Tripp because he was here now. To suggest that wasn't a perfect arrangement was thinking something about Tripp that I didn't feel. It was a great idea and a great message Bristol was sending out to the world and all the young kids. It wasn't easy raising a baby. I did think there were more realistic options, even if I didn't pay attention myself. Birth control. Condoms.

Not that we observed such precautions on Turnagain Street. Why not? Bristol didn't want me to, loved the idea of another baby. Did I really go along? Again? Duh.

There was another issue. We needed to tell Bristol's parents we were together. It was the *I'm pregnant* scene all over again. We even had Willow—the one-man Palin police, who slept over sometimes and knew her sister and I were a couple—once again pushing us to come clean or she'd tell.

She might have been a pain in the ass but she sure kept everyone honest. I thought that Bristol and I should take the baby and drive to Wasilla and spit it out, face-to-face. At least that's what I said; I was pretty sure my babe wouldn't want to do that. I wasn't really interested in dealing with Todd in person.

Bristol opted to open communications with her mother in their usual manner, which also happened to be the most distant and safest way. We were lying in bed when Bristol texted Sarah.

Levi is staying here. We R together again.

The pause lasted about an hour, or so it seemed. Probably ten minutes as Bristol's message filtered throughout the Palin household.

Willow, who told her parents she already knew, texted to her parents, Be nice.

Britta, Track's longtime girlfriend, joined Willow, tried to keep everyone moving in a positive direction.

Sarah. Todd. They couldn't believe it. Track climbed on, even though he already knew about me and Bristol. They all were taking turns texting away, dumping on Bristol, saying she was making a huge mistake. Track texted Bristol that I was an idiot.

Bristol texted back, U need to get over it; we r in love; we r getting married.

Two days later, Sarah and Todd were supposed to pick up Tripp for the weekend. Bristol got a text that morning. They wouldn't be coming.

Willow had planned to come along with them, then spend the weekend in Anchorage, at the condo. Her folks also refused to drive Willow, so Bristol went to Wasilla to pick her up.

When Bristol got back home, as soon as she saw me, she broke down. Before she was done, she was weeping in my arms. Willow, also shook up, took Tripp to his room to play as Bristol told me what had happened. She had driven down the Palins' driveway and stopped to turn off the engine. Before she had a chance, Willow threw open the door of the house and came running out, with her backpack over one shoulder.

Right behind her was Todd.

No, he yelled at Willow. I don't want you to go to that condo. Levi'll knock you up, too, just like he did Bristol.

I couldn't imagine my father ever saying such a thing to my sister. Todd wasn't through, as he turned to Bristol.

And you, he pointed at his oldest daughter. Falling for the first boy who sniffs up your skirt. What the fuck is wrong with you?

I was back at my place in Wasilla the next day, and Willow was back from Anchorage as well, at a friend's in my neighborhood. When Track came to pick up Willow, he drove by my house with his hand flat on his horn. *Honkkkk.*

Later that night, he called me. His phone was on speaker and he was trying to disguise his voice. *I'm gonna kill you,* he said in this scary tone. *Better watch outtttt. I know where you liiiiive.*

I laughed. Douche bag Track, I told my phone, come on over anytime. You, too, Sarah. Todd. I could just see them all sitting around. Who else was he playing to? Piper? Trig? Maybe I was nuts.

Sarah had a different approach toward me than Todd's. She set up a meeting. I didn't want to do it, not at her house, not unarmed. My dad offered to come with me, but we both knew I had to go alone.

When I arrived at the Palin house, I didn't walk in like I used to, back when Sarah was the only one home, and, later, back when I lived there.

This time, I knocked.

Todd came to the door. I have, he spit out, nothing fucking to say to you. Wait in your truck.

He was a hothead, swore a lot. I didn't think I'd ever heard Sarah swear. Todd made up for her share.

My appointment with Sarah was not the usual What are your intentions? How serious are you? She already had those answers; she had always known how I felt about her daughter. She might have wanted to ignore it, but she knew. No, what she wanted was an apology. For what, exactly? For all the true shit I'd said about her?

I told her I'd work on it.

I went back to Bristol in Anchorage and thought about it. An apology was due from me, not to Sarah but to Bristol—for the ugly war of words I hadn't been old or wise enough to ignore. I felt bad that Bristol had lost her dream. In a couple of weeks, when we would no longer be together, she would tell *People*:

> *If fame, money and my mom Sarah Palin's vice presidential campaign had not become part of my and Levi's lives, we'd already be happy living a simple life. I think Levi and I would be married. He would still have his job on the North Slope, and we'd be in a one-bedroom apartment, scraping by. . . . Levi and I are both Alaska-based, and I don't see us moving anywhere else.*

Amen.

But, for now, the dream wasn't gone. Not yet. We still had fourteen more days. As I sat hunched over the little living-room desk in the condo, working on my apology, someone—maybe Tank, my manager, who lived to create buzz—tipped off *US Weekly* that we were a couple again. Bloggers jumped on board, reported that neighbors knew I was at Bristol's at all hours.

I parked in the garage—but that hadn't worked for my dad, and it didn't work for me.

When I took Tripp for a walk, Bristol's neighbors always said hello to me, talked to Tripp. My presence was no secret.

Bristol blew up and blamed her favorite scapegoat—my sister—for a photo of my truck and Bristol's truck side by side at the condo that showed up all over the Net and in the press.

In the first place, Sadie was a photographer and would never have taken such a crummy shot. She also had no idea where the condo was; only Bristol's pals knew. What was the secret anyway, once Sarah and Todd had been told?

This idea that Sadie was somehow at fault for something stirred up all the old jealous feeling in Bristol. She was having a fit as I labored over how to word my not-so-sorry apology. She stopped long enough to hand me an envelope from her and Sarah's lawyer. It was meant to be my statement. A letter from Thomas Van Flein instructed me to sign it. My message, as Van Flein drafted it, was as stiff as his stationery:

> *Last year, after Bristol and I broke up, I was unhappy and a little angry. Unfortunately, against my better judgment, I publicly said things about the Palins that were not completely true. I have already privately apologized to Todd and Sarah. Since my statements were public, I owe it to the Palins to publicly apologize.*

What bullshit.

It had me saying I lied when I did not. I sat down,

changed words, added a phrase, worked at softening the falsehoods. It's not easy to write that you are sorry and at the same time say every damned thing you said was absolutely true. Before I finished, before I could send my version to Sarah and Van Flein, *People* had printed the attorney's words as mine, on July 6.

The Levi Johnston apology had another piece. I had no idea where it came from, these extra few sentences hooked on at the end:

> *So to the Palin family in general and to Sarah Palin in particular, please accept my regrets and forgive my youthful indiscretion. . . . I hope one day to restore your trust.*

People also printed a statement from Bristol. She didn't write it, didn't see it until it was published. Sarah must have remembered when the same number was pulled on her, when the McCainers ignored her corrections to the announcement that Bristol was pregnant—they just sent out what they wanted. She'd just done the same to me; and then to her daughter. *Too bad.*

> *Part of co-parenting is creating healthy and honest relationships between the parents. Tripp one day needs to know the truth and needs to know that even if a mistake is made the honorable thing to do is to own up to it.*

Double bullshit. Triple.

Sadie went ballistic. She wrote on her blog that she was shocked by my apology, that Bristol always meant to get pregnant—and that I was the one getting screwed. It's all wrong, she said.

Bristol had loved to kid around when she was at my house, tell my mom and sister that she was going to have a baby. Then laugh and tell them she was fooling—that time.

Bristol was incensed by Sadie's comments. She forbade me to talk to my flesh and blood. I wasn't to see her either.

Okay, Bristol. Whatever.

Once again, it wasn't just my sister who had to be shunned. Bristol didn't want me to see my friends—my family of friends—either. Tyson, Dominic, Derek, Chad, Mark, Crosby. The guys I grew up with.

Right, Bristol.

This is great, Tank said. We'll sell the engagement, the wedding, the baby. A reality show—ten episodes. He shared his thoughts with the media.

Thomas Van Flein announced that there would be no reality show.

I should maybe have listened to my baby sister, who had it right. Then I wouldn't have had to say confusing crap like I did to Betty Nguyen on *The Early Show* over a month later as I stammered, trying to explain away the Van Flein apology.

Betty, I lied when I said I lied.

I sounded like a horse's ass. I was the laughingstock of the country—anyone who cared anyway. I think even Betty smirked. Maybe not. She's a nice lady. Worse, she was probably pitying my sorry ass.

That conversation with Betty on *The Early Show* wouldn't take place until August. It was July, and for Bristol and me things were . . . okay. During the time we'd been apart, cracks had developed in my vision of her as a goddess who could do no wrong—and I didn't know what to do to repair them. I was there, though, 100 percent for Tripp. I would tell *US Weekly* how bad I felt, as a father, missing such milestones as his first word and first steps. I'd not been there and I can't change that. More important, I'm here now, for Bristol and Tripp, and I'm going to make it right. I love them both very much.

That was true. Nothing on earth compared with the delight I felt when the three of us were in bed together, with the little one hunkered down between us. No matter what happened in the future, I knew then, and now, that that was a joy I'd always hold on to.

Before speaking to *US Weekly*—before the engagement story—I proposed to Bristol. We already knew we were getting hitched, and I thought it would be a nice touch to formalize it, to get down on one knee. I did do that, in our bedroom. The bed where Bristol had sat down was covered with a heart of rose petals. I worked on that goddamned heart for an hour, to get it symmetrical. I had cleaned out the supply at Safeway's floral section, had flowers all over the place—a throwback to our wedding plans in the Rose Garden in Washington, and then the substitute wedding dream in the Palins' yard alongside Lake Lucille. I still want roses, Bristol had said after it was the Bidens and not the Palins moving to D.C. Lots.

This was going to be our third try at a wedding. Three's good.

For rings as well. Rings especially.

I had gone to Fred Meyer and checked out their engagement-ring selection at the affordable-jewelry showcase. I chose the one that best matched the description Bristol had given me.

Wrong.

Back to the store again, this time with my sister. Although Bristol snarled whenever I mentioned Sadie, they had at some point discussed engagement rings, even looked at them together. Sadie knew what Bristol had in mind.

The sales slip somehow had Sadie's name on it along with mine. The ring might have been perfect; I think it was. When Bristol saw the name Mercede Johnston, there was no way it could be right.

On my way back to Fred Meyer, alone this time, I was beginning to say to myself that, if this didn't do it, I needed to reassess. Particularly after Bristol had shouted after me as I went out the door, *I bet you even screw your sister!*

A little less politely actually. A twisted strain of suspicion coursed through Palin veins. I never got over that particular nastiness. What a rude, disgusting, unpleasant, disrespectful thing to say about me, my sister, my whole family. It was sad, from someone whose relatives, as they chirped about values, had no use for one another, no love, no sensitivity. Oh, they harped on it, wrote about it, but it wasn't there. Not the kind of love my family and I had for one another.

Even when I was wishing my sister would button her lip.

I still loved Bristol after her outburst. Just a little bit less. I told myself she didn't mean it; it was just her way to lash out. The thing about small hurts is that, when you aren't even looking, they pile up into one large, open boil, draining pus, unable to ever close again.

16

A Green-Eyed Monster

We still were on course. The next step was for the parents of the bride to make the engagement announcement, place it in the local paper with a couples photo. Bristol and I had not forgotten Todd and Sarah's reaction to the text about our getting together again. We decided to control the news ourselves—and make some money. We knew we were a commodity and had no problem profiting from that. We had contacted *US Weekly* and agreed to let them interview and film the happy couple and Tripp in the condo. For $300,000.

The Palin family attorney would handle the contract. Van Flein's lips were sealed; he promised not to share this information with his primary client, Sarah. Now he was working for Bristol as well as me.

Sort of.

Bristol and I were to split the proceeds. Fifty-fifty. I didn't get this; why not place the $300,000 into a joint account? When the contract was put before me after being run by Rex as well, I sat down and read it. The deal had changed. Now it was Bristol 75 with me getting 25 percent. Why did it matter, Bristol chirped, who got what money? We'd soon be married and sharing. She didn't say she was in on this, and I never did know who told Mr. Van Flein to alter the contract. Sarah was supposed to be out of the loop, yet she was Bristol's mom and I would think that the attorney's first loyalty would be to her.

I was last in the legal food chain.

No adult was there protecting my interests, certainly not Thomas Van Flein. Well, Rex was, but he must have overlooked the new math.

As usual, I rolled over. Whatever.

The publication date for our engagement-announcement photo spread was July 14, and I didn't even share the information with my parents and my sister. My mother would be upset to learn of her son's engagement while in the checkout line at Carrs. My sister would tell me later that Mom cried in the car on the way home and was sniffling when I spoke to her an hour later. This was the mother who got teary-eyed when her little boy took Michelle out on his first real date.

Back in the sixth grade, I got up the guts to ask out a girl named Michelle.

Since fourth grade, I'd always had a girlfriend. This was different—an actual date, going somewhere. Michelle was blonde, talkative, and giggly. Very friendly, too. I was enchanted. My mother already knew her, through my kid sister.

When my mom and I picked her up at her house in our red Taurus, there was this awkward silence. I couldn't think of a thing to say! Mom, always the one to save my neck, made some kind of joke. That broke the ice, and Michelle and I started talking at the same time.

When Mom dropped us off at the movies, she said she'd be back to pick us up before the movie got out. As Michelle and I came out of the darkness, my eyes searched for our red car. I was somehow worried that we'd have to wait; I don't know why. My parents could be counted on to do whatever it was they said they'd do.

Our Taurus was there, parked, waiting for us. We got in, and Michelle and I, sitting together in the back seat, started to chomp on our leftover handfuls of Skittles that I'd bought. We chatted and laughed the whole way home. I thought it was awesome.

I remember Mom asking me, after I'd walked Michelle to her front door, then climbed into the front seat of our car:

How was your first date, Levi?

It was great!

I noticed that Mom was crying. Back then, I couldn't understand why. Now, as a parent myself, I realize that it was emotional for her to see her baby boy out on his first date.

Or getting married.

———

Dad was relaxed about the engagement. Well, okay, Son. If that's what you want.

The Palin set of parents got the news when their phones started vibrating at 4:00 a.m.—eight o'clock East Coast time. We knew it would tick them off, to find out that way—but we'd signed an exclusivity agreement and could not tell anyone.

Next, the Palin parents saw the spread on TV. Their response, a public statement, had a different tone from the reaction I got from my family.

> *Bristol at 19 is now a young adult. We obviously want what's best for our children. Bristol believes in redemption and forgiveness to a degree most of us struggle to put in practice in our daily lives.*

A newscaster wanted to know if I'd asked Todd for Bristol's hand. I almost choked.

The Palins turned out to be right in their opposition to my being a part of Bristol's life. A mere four weeks after Tom Van Flein's release of my apology that he wrote, a new wave of shit hit the air. The stories seemed to break at the same time, one on top of the other. They were so absurd, so comical, that I laughed. Then I thought I heard some other sound, more like cackling. A murder of ravens—tricksters—trailing me, pulling strings? I looked at the sky. Nothing.

To Bristol, the most possessive human being on earth, it was no laughing matter.

Lanesia Garcia was pregnant, the media screamed, and I was the baby daddy.

Now who the hell put this stuff out? We grew up in a small town where everybody knew everyone else's business. Who would have a motive? Who wanted us apart?

Bristol believed it. She was furious. I had gotten someone else pregnant. I'm like, I am not even going to fight with you about this.

I had had a girlfriend, Lanesia Garcia, when I was a little kid, back in the Wasilla Middle School. Eighth grade, for Christ's sake. She was the prettiest girl in the school and the perkiest. If she came to my house, she'd set herself down in the living room or kitchen—wherever Mom was—and chat her up. My mom was crazy about this cutie-pie.

So was I. In the fucking eighth grade.

When I, as a freshman, started playing first line on the varsity hockey team, older girls began to chase me and I couldn't resist. So Lanesia and I broke up and we were no longer all that close.

In January of 2010, more than a year after Tripp was born and I'd moved out of the Palin house, I did hook up with Lanesia for one short night. Six months later, the international media community was announcing that Lanesia was pregnant with my child. *She* announced that she was barely pregnant—and the father of the child was her longtime boyfriend, and she had no fucking idea why anyone was connecting her to Levi Johnston at this point.

She called me and said I needed to clean up this mess.

A second reason why this baby could not be mine, as if another reason were needed, was that I'd used protection. Thank you, Wonderful Pistachios.

I'd just about convinced Bristol to call Lanesia and her boyfriend herself when the second bombshell landed in our laps.

This new gossip had it that I had told Bristol a lie. According to the rags and every damn blog in America, I had said that I was going to a California gun show—probably the state that has the most restrictive laws controlling the purchase and sale of firearms, if they even have gun shows there. Bristol knew I hadn't said that, but you have to understand that, even when you are the focus of all these stories, it's hard to keep them straight. So here's Bristol, who knows I never told her anything about any gun show or hunting show, and she's telling the press that I had said that, and it was a lie. Well, it sure as hell wasn't true! But what also wasn't true was that I said it. Does this have a familiar ring?—I would soon be explaining to Betty Nguyen that I'd lied in my apology to Sarah when I said I lied, in the apology I hadn't made.

I had lied this time, about going to a gun show, said the press, because I was really going to the lower forty-eight to see my new lover, to make a porn video.

I had been planning to go to California. I had committed to doing a music video with singer Brittani Senser. I thought videos might be a new income stream. This all was set up before Bristol and I got back together. I had told her about it, but it didn't seem to register with her until it was reported that there would be a steamy sex scene, and more. Then someone wrote that the video was meant to mock the Sarah-Bristol mother-daughter relationship. Like this was definitely the point? Like the song was written by Brittani with those two Palin females in mind? The Palins think everything is about them, including this damn video—so how could I win this battle? It wasn't going to happen.

Okay, Bristol. I won't do the video.

Who had floated that idea out there? Who knew that Bristol got green with jealousy? Or was it envy? I do not know. Who wanted us apart?

Three months after Bristol and I were history, the video would be on YouTube, on October 14. The least my ex-fiancée could have done, once she saw it, was to call up and apologize. In a beautiful scene at the end, I was standing in the rain, which was really garden hoses showering me from above. The mother—and her daughter—were inside reconnecting as I stood outside getting dumped on. You know, maybe it *was* about us after all.

As I had tried to explain to Bristol, the video's song was "After Love." It wasn't porn for Christ's sake. It was a love story. Sex? Yeah, it had a bedroom scene like in lots of PG-13 movies. I would wear boxer shorts under the sheet.

I was surprised, actually, when I was asked to take my shirt off. There was nothing but kissing. The suggestion was clear; these would be two people in love. Big deal.

Yes, said my Bristol. *Big fucking deal.* She yelled just that at the top of her lungs.

At least she didn't blame my sister.

I said to Bristol, Let me understand. We are splitting up because Lanesia got herself pregnant by someone, and because I never said I was going to a California gun show when I was really making a porn flick, which won't be a porn flick, and that I had told you about anyway?

There's more, she said. You also haven't done as I asked. I wanted you to use Van Flein, get rid of Rex and Tank. They didn't like Sarah, and Rex had bad-mouthed her, said Bristol. Rex had said that Bristol wanted me to be like Todd, hanging out in the background while she did the running around.

That seemed accurate to me.

Tank had chimed in, reporting to the media that Bristol was just being Bristol. What the hell did that mean anyway? I was betting I'd be credited with that quote.

I was thinking the best thing I could do was to go fishing.

Bristol's plan for our life together was that I would work on the oil patch as she continued to represent Candie's . . . once we were married. I had trouble understanding how she'd present a negative picture to the teens of the world with a husband, a nice house, and plenty of cash on hand.

She was already set up to be on *Dancing with the Stars*. As she did the show, I would work on the Slope, was her plan—taking care of Tripp in between.

Actually, it didn't sound all that bad. It was just that I wasn't about to give up Rex and Tank, and what had been set up, until I was sure everything was going to work out with Bristol. For now, we had separate checking accounts—Rex handled mine. I had no idea what her deal was. She'd never told me.

It went on for several days. When her mom would call, Bristol would take the phone into another room. They were scheming. Where was Sarah when her daughter needed her for a positive reason?

We weren't getting anywhere. If anything, things were going downhill. Half the time I had no idea what Bristol was yelling about.

I think she got that temper from her father. He's not there—until something sets him off. Attack him, his wife, his family? He's crazed. Otherwise, he's snow machining.

When Bristol got going, it was senseless to try to get a word in edgewise. I once suggested she get her blood pressure checked. That went over well.

Tripp's eyes, the same blue as his grandpa Todd's, were big as he stood there, looking on and listening.

I ended it. I walked out the door, got in my truck, and drove. I was ending my life with Tripp, too, the kind where you lived with your kid. I knew it; I didn't see what else I could do. Bristol, or someone, would release a statement saying she'd been played. Maybe we had both been played. Had the adults won once again?

We'd split the cash we'd gotten for the engagement. She kept three-quarters and gave me one-fourth.

After the blowup, reported around the world for God's sake, Brittani Senser or perhaps her manager decided to release a quote that her song and video did play in with my life. Oh, really? Some people will do and say anything for PR.

I loved that video. It was great fun to make and a new experience for me. I learned a lot about the process, including that I wasn't actor material. No one called saying I was perfect for a remake of *Red River*.

Bristol made her own video with Static Cycle, an Alaska progressive rock band. In it, she caressed an ice phallus, with a rose frozen inside.

Bristol announced—or Van Flein or Sarah's machine did—that she expected the split would get nasty. What an odd comment. The press was told that she said her family had seen many people say and do many things to cash in on the Palin name. Sometimes that greed clouded good judgment and the truth.

Bristol told *People* that she felt sure she'd find another husband and father for Tripp, someone who had religious beliefs—and, of course, a good family.

Bullying my flesh and blood again. They couldn't seem to stop keeping alive that dead horse. They force-fed it grain and poured water down its throat regularly. Where did this meanness come from? I wondered if their own screwed-up situation drove them to attack my tight-knit caring, loving, though-not-problem-free relatives. Yes, jealousy.

Bristol may have found religion; okay, she might find a husband. Tripp already had a dad, and she wasn't going to replace me just like that. I had to keep reminding myself that Van Flein had probably written that one also. It did have the feeling of a daughter being under her mother's thumb.

Everyone was headed for Wasilla. Only a year and a half before, Bristol and I had split up for the first time—little more than a month after Tripp was born. I was packing once again my bivvy sacks, throwing my crap into my truck, and kissing my son good-bye. I wondered if this was how my grandpa Joel felt, after the second time he and my grandma called it quits. The difference there was that Grandpa Joel kept the kids, my dad and his sister, Rene. So maybe I needed to channel my grandmother instead.

I was gone on a Tuesday. I heard later that Bristol was out of Anchorage the following day, August 4, the same day her condo was placed on the market. She was back in the house on the lake, along with Tripp and his Mommy Sarah.

I dumped my stuff at my mommy's as well, staying with her and my sister until I rented my own house.

My buddy Dom, who worked on the Slope, moved in with me and we split the rent. I set up the third bedroom for Tripp, and for me. Full of toys. And, finally, got my own shit put away.

That was when I realized that the few photos I had of me and Bristol were gone. I only had had, maybe, five. Even right after she gave birth, she didn't want to be photographed with Tripp. I did have some, though, that she had approved of, that she didn't rip up. Not anymore. The envelope where I kept them was gone. I had no pictures of the two of us at all. It was as if four years of my life never happened.

I asked her about it once, when I met her to get Tripp and, behind his head, she gave me the bird.

To get some buzz going about the video, Brittani and her team had wanted me to escort her to the Teen Choice Awards. I'd never gotten up the nerve to mention this to Bristol when we were together. She would have gone off on a tear. About nothing, since I wasn't planning on doing it.

Things had changed.

Nothing could have matched the time Kathy Griffin had shown me the ropes the year before. I'd been awestruck—I did as I was instructed, pretty much kept quiet and watched. I learned from Kathy. This time, with Brittani, I knew how to handle the press. People recognized me. I shook hands; I signed autographs. I needed

Tank's Sharpie! I did all the talking. I felt, for the first time, comfortable in the showbiz arena.

My split with Bristol made me a hotter commodity. My face, my quotes—even though they weren't mine and were damaging—were out there. I became a punch line for late-night TV. It had the same effect on Bristol. She cut me out of her life and danced off with the stars.

I wished I'd have known. She'd left Wasilla without feeling like it was information she needed to share. We'd agreed that I'd see my little guy every day, every week, whenever I wanted. She wanted me to; she knew it was good for Tripp. That was unrealistic on both our parts, but I did expect his mom to keep in touch about where he might be, or not be. He's my kid!

I had gone to L.A. myself for a few days. I'd texted Bristol telling her I'd be gone and would be back to see Tripp over the weekend. No response, but I didn't really think about it, hadn't yet learned that, when she didn't text back, it meant Tripp wasn't in Wasilla.

Tank was saying we should stay in L.A. for a month or so, line up gigs. I didn't want to miss seeing Tripp, so we went back home. That's when I found out Bristol had gone into rehearsal for *DWTS*—trailing Tripp and a nanny—for three months. In L.A.

My overextended lawyer said he'd bring it all up at the next court appearance, in a couple of months.

As for Bristol and *DWTS*, Tank said I had turned down an earlier offer from them. I think that might have been bullshit. Truth, lies—they seemed to be a piece of my life.

Tank also told the press I was shopping a book and a reality show.

Before returning to Alaska after my second appearance at the Teen Choice Awards, I got together with Stone & Company. Canaan Rubin, my L.A. producer friend who had come to Wasilla with a camera crew to film my son's first birthday for *ET*, now was with Stone. He and Tank and Scott Stone—along with his assistant—had brainstormed, trying to come up with a theme that would make us all some money and maybe lift my spirits.

Bad Boys of Alaska? A dating show like *Bachelor*, with an Alaskan twist? That's when Canaan's assistant hit upon an idea they all thought was brilliant. I could throw my hat in the ring and run for the mayor's seat in Wasilla. Following in Sarah's footsteps. Tank said if I was mayor for a while, maybe I could be governor.

I thought, How about my getting as far away from the Palins as I could?

I said it was absolutely a terrible, horrible idea. I said no, it wouldn't fly. I couldn't see myself doing that.

My campaign, they went on, would be the basis for a reality show. They decided to call it *Loving Levi*—a strange choice given the recent poll that suggested a title like

Loathing Levi would be more accurate. Given the news coverage I was getting since my second breakup, what about *Laughing at Levi*?

The actual mayor of Wasilla, Verne Rupright, would point out that my campaign was off to a bad start:

> *It's a little early to declare for an election in 2011. Usually, most wait until the year the seat is up. But since I'm nearly old enough to be Levi's grandfather, I think it would be wise for him to get a high school diploma and keep his clothes on. The voters like that!*

I could have listened to Mayor Rupright's advice, who *was* old enough to be my grandfather as far as I can tell but, before I could think, let alone make sure my clothes were in place, Tank and Canaan told *Variety* I was pitching a reality show. If Tank continued in his usual pattern, we could also name it *Leaking Levi*.

My dad, hearing about all this, thought it sounded as crazy as I did and was leaving a hundred voice mails a day. My mother was texting a thousand times a day. They wanted to understand and know every little thing. If I gave them something, they needed to know everything. Tank and Rex were running things, I tried to tell them, helping me out. I didn't need to discuss everything. It was about becoming an adult, moving away from your ma and pa. It wasn't that I loved them less. In fact, with a child of my own, I felt more for them than I ever did.

I knew deep down that my folks were right to be concerned. I didn't know what this was all about, didn't have a plan. I was twenty, sitting around in Wasilla, Alaska, listening to people who said that they knew what was best for me. But did they really? Was making money always best?

Were Bristol's people giving her the same advice?

The public response to *Loving Levi* was what you'd expect. I was arrogant, unprepared, and hadn't earned my chance for either a reality show or a mayoral run. I felt out of my depth, just a little, especially when Tank explained to CBS News:

> *People questioned Jesus Christ, too, so I definitely don't care about these mere mortals questioning Levi Johnston. . . . People can question whatever they want. I mean, he's got to keep on doing his own thing. He was good to do this even if this wasn't a reality show.*

It was a lot like the situation when Thomas Van Flein—or Sarah?—released my apology in words that weren't mine. Once it was out there, I couldn't bring it back. Jesus! But with Tank you had to take the good with the crazy.

I knew wolf, caribou, musk ox. Not public relations, not publicity, not fame, and not politics. Including the mayor's seat. *Loving Levi* now had assumed a life of its own. Tank was out of control. He always had been. He was impossible. At the start, he was definitely dumber than I was when it came to Hollywood shit. When I saw something on

TV, I paid attention. By now, he'd improved, was smarter, savvy. I thought he was figuring it all out, just as I was. I continued to rely on him. I felt that I still needed a buffer. I knew that half the time his voice mail would be full, that he didn't respond to e-mail, or texts. Who else would deal with it all if he wasn't there? Me?

He announced he was both my campaign manager and the manager of my film life. I had no idea if he realized the need for raising money for my campaign, or about conflicting film and campaign schedules. The show was supposed to chronicle my political run along with my search for love. I didn't live within the city limits. I sure as hell didn't know anything about city ordinances or a comprehensive plan.

Sarah mocked the mayoral concept; so did Bristol, who had in fact loved Levi. She told Jay Leno that she didn't know I had such aspirations, but she was pleased to hear that I was looking for steady employment. Bristol, babe, I'm paying you $1,750 a month; what is it you are trying to do exactly? My film-career manager, Tank, told the press, Levi's going to take political college courses. He's going to really deal with the issues.

God. I was embarrassed. Like I usually did when I felt uneasy, I told myself I didn't care.

The production company was good to go with the *Loving Levi* concept. They were planning to shoot a pilot in Wasilla and wanted to include some footage shot in L.A.

Tank and I flew down, and we and the crew headed for the streets around Rodeo Drive and trolled. All they had to do was to aim a camera at me and the paps came out from behind the palm trees. Stone had me situated as they wished. The star of *Loving Levi* was in fact a star, adored wherever he went. Here was the proof.

Canaan released the game plan to the media.

The docu-soap will follow the ever controversial, headline making, matinee idol, handsome father of one as he embarks on a run for mayor of Wasilla, Alaska. . . . [The] series will chronicle a "no-holds-barred" period in Levi's tumultuous life; co-raising his son Tripp, looking for love, and taking care of business for his fellow Wasillians. He will give us a real inside look into who he is as a father, a skilled hunter, an avid dirt biker, and of course his journey down the road of small town politics—right after he gets his high school diploma. Levi thinks he can take the office by representing the real citizens of Wasilla. If elected, Levi promises to serve his full term. Tank Jones will serve as Levi's campaign manager.

While I was in California, I gave a talk to a film class at the University of California at Los Angeles. What an experience. Me, with no high school diploma, in front of this group of UCLA students, interested in what I had to say, my experiences. I told them where I came from and what I was doing now. I told them what I hoped to do in the future. We followed this with questions, and suggestions about making *Loving Levi* a success.

They had come up with some clever ideas, but I never got to try out any of them. My talk was the most that came from the *Loving Levi* grand plan. Tank told people a month later that the producers felt that the title *Tank and Levi* would work better. No shame. It is always balls to the wall with him. One thing doesn't work out, he is on to the next. The plan was, he said, to take me out on the streets of Anchorage and teach me how to be a private investigator. I thought about suggesting we get Willow to team up with us, at least on paternity cases.

Being trained as a PI might have been a helpful skill for me, too. Maybe I could find Bristol and see Tripp. He might be just around the corner in Wasilla, but it was as if he were a million miles away. Bristol was acting completely different from the way she was when we were together in the condo. She'd reverted to acting the way she had when we broke up the first time.

One day when I was talking to Bristol on the phone, trying to suggest a regular permanent arrangement to pick up my boy that she might agree to, she said something that knocked the wind out of me.

I don't know if Tripp should have your last name.

I was like, What?!??

Who does something like that to a father? Sometimes there's one thing that can, in just one moment, change how you feel about someone. This was the turning point

FPO

IN THE SUPERIOR COURT FOR THE STATE OF ALASKA

THIRD JUDICIAL DISTRICT AT PALMER

BRISTOL PALIN,)
)
Petitioner,)
)
vs.)
)
LEVI JOHNSTON,)
) Case No. 3PA-09-2261CI
Respondent.)

STIPULATION REGARDING CUSTODY AND CHILD SUPPORT

The parties, through counsel, hereby stipulate and agree to the following with regards to the parties' minor child, Tripp E. Johnston-Palin, born December 27, 2008:

1.   This child has lived in Alaska for at least six months immediately before the complaint was filed in this action, and the court has jurisdiction over this child.

2.   Legal custody of the child will be awarded to the parties jointly, however if the parties cannot, after consultation between them, decide on an issue, Bristol Palin shall make the final decision.

for me. A second one, actually. I saw it as a second insult to that abscess I worried about, that had begun to fester. It wasn't yet one large, open wound, draining pus. Once that happened, it would never heal.

From then on, Bristol was terrible in my eyes. Later that month, she and I agreed in writing—*stipulated* was the word the lawyers used—that, while Tripp lived with Bristol, I could see my son at least two days a week. This was a new and wonderful promise. Bristol had signed and I signed right below her signature—and so did our attorneys. I didn't notice—and I assumed Rex didn't either—that the child involved in *Palin v. Johnston* had a different name from the one he was born with. How the hell could I have missed that? Did I even read it? It was six pages long, and if I did more than just sign it when it was placed under my nose, I probably ignored that first introductory page.

It was only seven o'clock and I hadn't eaten dinner. I realized I had no appetite and went to bed, once again wrapped in my protection gear—my camo quilt.

The next morning, before I had time to remember how dismal I found my life, I was jolted awake by a squeal and the tinkle of a bell. It took me a fraction of a second to realize what was going on. My nutty cat, Trigger, who had left the shelter to join my household a couple of weeks earlier, liked Tripp's toys. Never, ever had either Dom or I been able to catch him at it, but he was the culprit. No question.

When I dragged myself out from under my covering, I walked toward Tripp's room. There was Trigger, in the doorway, with Tripp's SpongeBob SquarePants between his front paws. Nowhere near the fire truck. Trigger had that look he would get if I tried to feed him a piece of celery. *What the hell are you doing, buddy?*

At least someone was playing with the toys in that room. As I went toward the kitchen, SpongeBob squeaked.

I'd set the room up with a junior bed in the middle for naps, one of those things that was styled to be a car. With *Cars* sheets. Tripp giggled at it or maybe just liked to get me to laugh.

On those times, though, that Tripp was with me, his real interest was in his miniature Fairbanks Ice Dogs hockey stick. His favorite puck would be the cat if he could ever catch him.

Instead, I used a tennis ball to show my son the secrets of stick handling, how to deke me out. He could just keep his balance swinging it around; but he loved it. I had stowed in the closet, next to the little flannel shirts, a set of big-boy skates, the smallest size CCM makes—the real deal—not those strap-ons with double runners.

Tomorrow was supposed to be my day with Tripp. Bristol had been cagey on the phone before she brought up changing Tripp's last name. I was betting they were gone, out of state. In New York? L.A.? They could have been in Wasilla at the Palin home, in Bristol's apartment in the same outbuilding as Sarah's Fox studio. Maybe just Bristol was off somewhere, leaving Tripp behind. We were right back where we'd been after our first breakup. And I still hadn't done a good job figuring it all out.

I flipped on some country. A Waylon Jennings ballad filled my house. He sounded like he might have been in an even bigger mess than me. Now he was singing, *Where stars were for shining in the Arizona sky / And music meant more than fortune or fame. . . .*

Tripp could have been in Arizona. I had found out from my dad that Bristol had bought a house there. He caught her being interviewed on TV.

My lawyer, Rex, had said at the time that he was on it. I heard no more. It wasn't his fault. It had all just become too much. All the bullshit was static in my head.

Bristol, Dad said, had stumbled over her words when questioned about Tripp's seeing his dad since she'd moved to Maricopa—then added that she'd bring my son to me in Alaska whenever I wanted. How would that work, Bristol, when you never told me he was leaving and, once gone, you didn't respond to my texts or calls? I wasn't sure I'd want to put the kid through those endless hours of travel anyway.

I was sure she wouldn't even remember having said it. It was like her explanation for Tripp's name choice. Total makeup. I couldn't even remember what the hell she'd said and I bet she'd forgotten, too. No one has a good enough memory to make a good liar.

Johnston men don't want to see themselves as victims, but it was humiliating to have no presence in your child's life. I was beginning to realize that, no matter what the issue, when it came to Tripp, I was going to lose. When this happened over and over and you knew the outcome wouldn't get any better for you or for your kid, it was easy to wimp out, to stop fighting. I wasn't proud of this, but that's where I was beginning to see myself ending up.

My boy was the anchor of my schedule. I tried to keep open the days I belonged to him. That meant I turned down work. I sat around watching the dishes dry. I'd run a load through the washer. Vacuum. My house was neat, maybe too neat.

I wouldn't let myself start texting and calling—hoping this was the time I'd get an answer—for Saturday, the second day in the week I was allowed to see Tripp.

I knew I wouldn't be able to help myself. I wanted to see him.

Are you going to be here?

OK if I pick up Tripp at 9?

Can I see my boy, please?

I've been waiting, B, for any response at all for 32 hrs.

It's my time to see my son; what's your plan?

Where the fuck is T?!

I knew if I let it get to me, then I'd have no control at all.

It's not a good time for me, she'd text back. Maybe this afternoon; I'll call U.

All along, before we had gotten back together and since

then, I'd get the rare call from Bristol, who wanted to share the usual things dads and moms smile over together. Tripp just jumped off something. He just said thus and so. Bristol knew we both felt the same about Tripp.

Then, with no warning, she'd get ugly.

I saw a T-shirt once that said THE OLDER I GET, THE MORE I'M LIKE MY MOTHER.

In a way I hated that bedroom. The Pampers in the middle of the changing pad in the corner are too small for him now. I should have gotten rid of them, but I just couldn't. That would mean his infancy was over and I'd not been there for him for most of it. Bristol was a wonderful mom to him, but, still, I was, once again, worried about how my son was handling life without me.

The rare times I had him made me feel better about this concern. Tripp would at first cry for Bristol. I'd put him in the truck and shut the door until she walked away. Then he was good to go—a happy little baby. I took him to see my parents and sister. We visited aunts, uncles, and cousins. By the time we were ready to have fun in his little bedroom, it was almost time to get him to his mom. He was always all smiles and sleepy as I handed him over.

I needed to do something other than mope. I decided to hop in my truck, take a ride to nowhere. That's when I heard a song—on my favorite country station, 107.5

KASH Country—promo'd: "Levi Johnston's Blues," written by Nick Hornby with Ben Folds, a balladeer. I knew about it, but had never heard it. Now I did.

I couldn't keep driving. I pulled off the road, and as I began to chuckle, my mood changed. So clever; I was laughing my ass off. I was singing the chorus along with Ben by the time it ended. I knew he was making fun of me. I realized that when there wasn't anything you could do but cry, it was time to laugh.

Woke up this morning, what do I see?
Three thousand cameras, pointing at me
Dude says, You Levi? I'm like, Yes, that's me, sir!
Well, you've knocked up the VP nominee's daughter

So I tell him, No, you got it wrong, mister
Already with a girl, and her name's Bristol
They all laugh and say, Where you been, sonny?
Your mother-in-law's a heartbeat from the presidency

I say, Mother-in-law? No, we ain't getting married
They say, You will be soon, boy, she just announced it
I get on my dirt bike, ride to my girl's home
I'm gonna lay down the law, tell her what's going on

CHORUS:
I'm a fuckin' redneck, I live to hang out with the boys
Play some hockey, do some fishing, kill some moose

I like to shoot the shit and do some chillin', I guess
Ya fuck with me and I'll kick your ass

So we talk and it turns out we don't believe in abortion
And sex outside marriage is against our religion
And when I try to tell them I'm eighteen years old
They say, Levi, it's too late, you gotta do as you're told

CHORUS:
I'm a fuckin' redneck, I live to hang out with the boys
Get on my snowboard, do some fishing, kill some moose
I like to shoot the shit and do some chillin', I guess
Ya fuck with me and I'll kick your ass

Folds had it right. How did he know? I was a redneck turned into something I wasn't sure anyone had put their finger on. Certainly not me. I.

17

Stalemate

It was the New Year—2011—when a friend texted me. Bristol had just posted a scary message:

Tripp Easton Mitchell Palin. Palin!!!!!

That sounded final. Changed. Done. The tweet, I found out, had been identified as a rumor and then a fact. It was all over the Internet. As I saw it, it had bad written all over it.

I left voice mail for Rex, drove into Anchorage a couple of days in a row and waited to see him, but I never caught up with him.

The next day, the same old friend, also a pal of Bristol's, texted me to listen to Bristol on the "Bob & Mark" radio show. Bob and Mark had been Sarah's biggest local radio boosters.

Bristol was nervous; I could tell.

Is the rumor, she was asked, about changing Tripp's last name true?

Bristol said, No. Unfortunately it's not true.

Levi has agreed to give you full custody in exchange for his no longer paying support?

It's a rumor. It sounds true.

She did, she said, want to get the issue of parental rights out of the way, and she had asked me many times to stop avoiding the ongoing custody battle.

What ongoing custody battle? What the hell was she talking about? We had signed an agreement to *share* custody. The only issue I could imagine was that Bristol had decided to change our agreement.

Bristol told Mark that I wouldn't sign over my rights to my son because it would look bad on paper.

Now that's a really shitty thing to say. Something her mother would come up with. She said I'd seen Tripp maybe three times, four hours each time, since *Dancing with the Stars* ended.

So true. God damn.

Seventeen days later, Bristol was out there again, talking to Gina Serpe of E! Online about her move to Arizona. Bristol told Gina she had full custody since Tripp's birth so her move to Arizona was no big deal.

Huh?

She then talked about her plan for me, in Alaska, and Tripp, in Arizona. Same bullshit. When Levi asks to see him, she explained, then I will make a trip to Alaska so that he could see him. . . . I would love for Levi to be a part of Tripp's everyday life, but I know that for Levi's lifestyle right now, that's just not a possibility.

She went on to imply that I wasn't able to provide stability.

Bristol said, Oh, yes, Levi and I are getting along. It's working out fine.

I got in my truck. Smoke was coming out of the exhaust as well as my ears as I drove, pulling up to one of our many lakes, one that I'd not looked out over in years, since the day Bristol had told her family we were back together.

On that day, close to a year ago, my cell had rung. I'd picked it up off the passenger seat and turned it on.

Levi, this is Sarah.

No shit.

Are you recording this?

Huh? What?

Don't lie to me. Are you taping this call? She sounded uptight. I could see her face coloring up.

No, Sarah. I'm not.

Are you positive? Tell me the truth.

Sarah, you called me. How could I be recording this? And why? I have no idea what the hell you want.

Sarah never had the balls to say anything to my face. She worked through others: her lawyer, her political associates, the media, the daughter. On the other hand, there was Bristol, screaming in my face. I didn't know which I had hated the most. Now I was no longer interested; I was done.

In the spring of 2011, my dad was in Yakima, Washington, at a car dealership. He was buying a new truck. When he gave the manager his name and then his Alaska address, the guy typed in the information, stopped, read what his screen said. He asked, Hey, you're not related to that Levi Johnston up there, are ya?

Dad said, Yes. He's my son.

The salesman looked at my father and said, It must have been quite a ride.

Wasilla, Alaska:
Happy Birthday to You . . .

The partygoers at the Chateau Nightclub aren't here for me. They're clubbers and see this night as an occasion to party. They dance into the night, sing and drink as I and my personal contingent of characters take the elevator upstairs to our rooms.

Along with Tank, I have two additional bodyguards:

six-foot-four Jungle, and Marvin, Tank's brother—the guy who just about killed me getting me fit for the *Playgirl* shoot.

The club gave me five first-class plane tickets along with hotel rooms and meals for all of us, and the $20,000. My friends are really along to have some fun. No one has attempted to kidnap me. No one has gotten all that close, other than girls wanting autographs and two mamas with iPhones, taking photos. And the blonde with the birthday card.

If someone did want to collect ransom, Jungle would be the man to stop them. He's this huge white guy. He talks rap; he's immaculate. Spectacular. Jungle's arms are the size of my legs. He's all solid meat with a soft overlay. That's his personality, too.

He works for Rex doing who knows what. Throwing people out third-floor windows maybe.

Jungle is sitting in one of the club's banquettes, between Marvin and Tank. They all are alert, watching for the strippers that aren't supposed to be here. I feel a little ridiculous with these three bouncer types. Like who am I that I need someone to protect me from the masses? I come across as a big ego: inflated, arrogant. I do get noticed a lot more when I am with Tank. Especially in Hollywood. They see a big black guy with me. I am all done up. I'm sitting there next to Tank and he's obviously a bodyguard. So people go, This white kid, he is somebody.

Still, the travel expense of extra people might make more sense as a deposit into my account. In the future, now that I'm a big boy, I need to decide if I can travel by myself, although I enjoy the company. This is work, though, not play.

Tank has always been there, by my side in Anchorage and the lower forty-eight. Before every show, he gets the questions they plan to ask on-air. Then he sits there, reads them to me, and I try out my answers.

He's more than a manager, my spokesperson. I'd come out of places like the CNN studio and there would be a bunch of cameras blocking my way to the limo. I just grab the back of Tank's shirt. The driver would spring open the door. I jump in and we are off.

I felt comfortable leaning on Rex and Tank. We went through a lot together. They were always looking out for the best thing for me, and I didn't think they'd ever screwed me over. I still trust them, but I've gotten smarter. I need to ask Team Levi to first run by me all leaks, tips, releases. I have a brain; I know what I want to say. I no longer am eighteen, nineteen, twenty. Rex and Tank always told me that they were interested in educating me so I could be out there on my own. I'm ready.

The club smells like they pour perfume into the air conditioner's circulating unit.

Happy birthday, Levi, everyone is wishing me. I smile, say, Thank you.

It isn't even my birthday.

———

My real twenty-first was in Wasilla, at home. That's the way I like it. No drinks. My new friend, Sunny, a low-key, honest, reasonable woman, gave me a framed photo of Duke, who is already hanging over the table, joining us as we sit down to eat. Sunny made a nice simple meal. Steak, asparagus, stuffed baked potato, salad, and, once I found it, a camo cake—mossy oak—with a mess of candles.

It was hilarious.

That's the extent of my partying. I don't like to raise hell; I rarely go to a restaurant. I used to, but not anymore. I've grown up to be the country boy I always was.

Within limits. Grandpa Joel's line about gay Paree isn't too far off. I don't see Wasilla the same after I've been in L.A. with its craziness. The 'Silla is home, but in a different way. I know more.

Back in Hollywood, shopping *Loving Levi: The Road to the Mayor's Office*, Canaan and Tank were talking like I was going to be a millionaire. A multimillionaire. They dragged me all over Holmby Hills and Brentwood, looking at estates for sale. I was sort of into it, but not really sold on it. I didn't see any forests, and I didn't see any animals other than sleeve dogs. Westies, Chihuahuas. Little ankle biters. When I told my father what we had been doing in Cali, and that Canaan was telling me I'd need to get my teeth veneered, I was set straight: If you do that, Dad told me, I'll knock them out of your mouth. Then his voice softened. That's not who you are, Son. Never forget where you come from.

The real me, who I am . . .

I'm a father, that's first, always. I'm an Alaskan, born and raised, and it's time for me to use my native and learned knowledge beyond the outdoors.

I know the art of patience as I sit in a tree stand for hours and even days, not talking to my companion, barely moving. A piece of that tolerance though, is recognizing when it's time to act. I've been wearing out the accepting angle and never getting to the point where I'm doing something about the situations I've managed to get myself into.

With the Palins, with the world outside the forest.

I'm at the point where I must control events and decisions that affect me and my son. Rex has told me for months that we need to get on board a family-law attorney. He's the first one to say that custody issues are not his expertise. I've started asking questions and calling family-law attorneys, getting a better understanding of what I need to do and who can best do it for me. That brings back my dad's wise words that when you don't know about something, you find an expert who does and you rely on them. I am moving forward on this front.

Tripp. Sometimes it's easier to wallow, to complain, to give up and accept the situation. I'm well aware that it's going to be tough to buck heads with the power of the

Palins' newfound fortune. The one thing I have going for me is that I'm on the right side. My new, more assertive stance will tick Mommy Sarah off. She's wired to win, not forgive and forget. Her political and personal strategy is to weaken and overwhelm her competition, clearing the field so that everyone left standing is more manageable. She's a master of carpet bombing, obliterating everything in her path.

Bristol has been turned into her lieutenant.

The number of attacks made on me, the many head-lined blitzes, had been successful. I'm an uneducated, nonworking stooge who is ignoring my kid, and I'm a deadbeat dad and a dope.

Some of their comments had backfired in the same way as Sarah's wringing of her hands after she was condemned for targeting Gabby Giffords. It was all about Sarah. People were being cruel to her.

Now, there is Bristol, the victim as well.

When I was eighteen, nineteen—when Sarah's assault began, she turned me into a sympathetic figure. Sarah had pounded me over the head so many times and in so many ways that some folks out there wondered, What did this poor kid do to deserve this?

I don't really care what she's done and what she's going to do. I no longer am going to respond—or not respond—as I've done in the past. I'm going to be the first to speak, loud and clear, when it injures my child's relationship with me. I am through being the target, in Sarah's crosshairs. I'm taking my life back.

I've jump-started the new me. I'm checking out the Wildlife Department's courses at the University of Alaska. I don't know what's going to happen to Levi Johnston in the world of entertainment, but if money comes in, it'll be saved to make real my lifelong dream. I see myself owning a guide business, along with my father and Dom. Dad would have to reactivate his pilot's license, and Dom wants to get one himself. We'd buy a couple of planes and I'd wait for my partners to bring in clients. I'd stay in the bush, with a big, long beard, showing people my Alaska, not Sarah Palin's.

I'm enrolled in an Anchorage aviation school; I will soon have earned my pilot's license.

My son will be a part of my life, wherever I am, wherever he and his mother settle. I have lessons and knowledge for Tripp that no one in the extended Palin family can offer. I remember one message I got from my father that I will pass on to my next generation—in the same way I learned it. . . .

Dad took me on a caribou hunt when I was eight years old. A buddy of his who was a pilot had spotted a large herd on the move—and where we could intercept them. Dad hustled me and some friends of his to get out there. It was the first time I drove my own four-wheeler on a real hunt. We came up this small rise, went over the top, looked into a valley that was a sea of caribou. Thousands!

We crept downslope and Dad set me up with my own rifle balanced on a tripod. I didn't realize until a couple of years ago that, when he took me hunting or fishing, my pop always made sure I would be successful so I would get the bug in me to want more and more and more.

The adults watched and waited for me to get my shot.

A huge male pushed by not more than twenty yards away. To an eight-year-old it was seriously close. The ground was shaking underneath my feet. The bull was followed by a few cows and some juveniles, getting smaller and smaller in line as they passed.

Crack!

I'd taken my shot. The herd took off and Dad took off after them. He ran a half mile after the bull I shot, assuming it was wounded but still able to move with the rest of the herd. My father wanted to get my bull and bring it back. The caribou Pops was chasing showed no sign of faltering, and when dad couldn't run anymore, he turned around and headed back, panting.

That's when he saw me and the others standing beside a dead caribou. He got closer and realized I had shot one of the smallest animals out there. A calf.

Son, Dad said to me, I thought you shot the big bull.

I shot the first one that stopped moving, I told him.

I didn't see it at the time, but my dad tells me all the guys were having a hell of a time keeping from guffawing. If I had noticed, that would've hurt my eight-year-old feelings. I thought I had done a damn good job.

Maybe they were laughing at Dad for trying to run down a healthy bull.

This taught me that there are different ways of looking at life, and different choices can be made based upon the same set of circumstances. If you do what you think is best, if you're true to yourself and where you come from and who you are, your choice will be the right one.

Like me, Tripp will be writing his own story with every breath and every choice. Like me, he can control the theme. This book was written for him, to read in a decade or two. Maybe he will pick it up again when he's a new father like me. Some passages I've written might make him sad; the truth does that sometimes. I do want him to be proud of me; it will help him to feel good about himself. We'll see how that goes. I know that, for my son and me to understand what happened over a few years' time when his families became household words, he needs to know who I was at the start, and how I grew to be an adult. That's about more than getting tall. Some call it a coming-of-age. When we were young, Tripp's mother and I promised to love each other forever. She had my baby and then we parted. What does that make me? A failure I guess. Mommy Sarah has said my son was a mistake; his mom, using softer words, suggested this was true, that we should learn from this. I want to be clear where I stand: my son, Tripp, is the best thing that ever happened to me, and I'd never throw in the towel when it comes to being his dad.

AND ONE MORE THING

Many have asked my reaction to Bristol's book and I am sure some of you have read *Deer in the Headlights* just to read my version of her events. I can't just make up a bunch of crap to match her lies. I can only give you what actually happened.

If that's how Bristol lost her virginity, I wasn't there. I never asked her when she did; that was her business.

She needed to explain away how this good Christian girl went astray—it's the first thing in her book—so she can make money as an abstinence spokesperson. Knowing now how her mother operates, and knowing what her daughter has learned at her mother's knee, I think that Bristol truly believes this is what happened.

We did camp with friends, well after she and I had forged a physical relationship in the spring of 2006. There *was* one afternoon when Bristol was running around, trying to line up alcohol for the night. I told her to forget it. She would lose her judgment when she drank. I mentioned

285

how one time when she was pregnant she asked for a wine cooler; I wouldn't let her do that. I don't know what else to say here. It's tough to talk about an event imagined in someone else's mind.

This is what the Palins do—seize the high ground and put others in a position where they have to respond when there's no way to do that.

The scene Bristol writes about, but leaves hanging—Track hunting me down to beat me up for violating his sister? Never happened. When Bristol and I got together again in 2010 and the whole Palin family was upset, Track did get angry and honked his horn while he twice drove by my house—but that was long after Tripp was born.

Bristol, like Mommy Sarah, blends events, locations, and truths to form her own carefully crafted reality much like *Sarah Palin's Alaska* and Sarah's own take on Paul Revere. The only difference between mother and daughter's spoon-fed moments is that Sarah's are delivered with a wink.

ACKNOWLEDGMENTS

My hunter's eyes and ears have recorded each moment, every experience, and my reactions to love and loss over the past six years. I recall how my family and friends were never shy when they saw I was headed down a dangerous path. Mom and Dad found a way to be supportive even when they thought I was crazy, and so did my sister Mercede. Most of my friends did the same—the ones who stuck by me. I thank them for that.

My lifelong friend, Dominick Nickels, was the truest of the true. He listened to me when I wanted to talk, ignored me when I didn't, and was there for me to turn to, to laugh with. Dom was part of the team that brought this book idea alive, along with my ghosts, James and Lois Cowan.

The Cowans had seen me out there on TV, read about me—and thought I was getting the shaft. I already knew I needed to do something before I was suffocated by half-truths and outright lies.

The Cowans and I—and Dom—spent time together

in Anchorage and Wasilla. We sat, drove, and walked; I talked, and the Cowans asked questions, mused, and recorded. We got beyond the ghostwriter-author work, and had conversations because we enjoyed spending time together. They acted like another couple of goddamned parents—pushing, prodding, expecting me to understand and explain a confusing series of events and a time when I often chose to bury my head under my quilt.

I wanted them identified as my coauthors. They felt one name should be on the jacket. It was my story, they said. Without the Cowans' patience and persistence, I still would be a deer in the headlights. They were unable to do anything about my god-awful spelling.

—Levi Johnston

This book was researched, organized, and written on a tight schedule. Our agent Robert Guinsler at Sterling Lord Literistic got the ball rolling and our time-pressed picky phenomenal editor, Matthew Benjamin, at Simon & Schuster's Touchstone imprint carried the play to the end. Beyond these pros, we thank transcriber, Dawny Mae Daly, attorney, Joel Sachs, literary muse, Mike Finney, Kathleen Baker of politicalgates.com, freelance editor, Cameron Cooke, and researcher, Alice Kehoe.

Physical and psychic energy was channeled by TOL Jones, Cody McCoy Leff, Hugh Van Dusen, Paula Norris, and Marny Heinen. Sizzle MacNelly contributed infectious laughter at both Levi's stories and our adventures. Our thanks to David Rich, Fred Cowan, and Hallie and Len Cowan; Jackie Lefferts, the Head Honcho, Michaele Cooke and Henry McDuff, Bonnie Staskowski, Margaret and Don Murray; and the Burke-Kennedy and Delahunt families.

We thank our newfound Wasilla pals who prefer to stay under the radar and who kept us full of Kaladi's mocha lattes and flush with contacts and sources.

—James and Lois Cowan